Ch[...]

Dear Joe & Kathleen

May this season be
your happiest + the
coming year your
best.

Love
Neil & Lois

IN HIS
HOLY
NAME

IN HIS HOLY NAME

Robert L. Millet
Joseph Fielding McConkie

BOOKCRAFT
Salt Lake City, Utah

Library of Congress Catalog Card Number: 88-72243

ISBN 0-88494-677-0

First Printing, 1988

Printed in the United States of America

And then the angel spake, saying:
. . . thou shalt do all that thou doest
in the name of the Son, and thou
shalt repent and call upon God in
the name of the Son forevermore.
—Moses 5:7-8

Praise ye the Lord. Praise, O ye servants of
the Lord, praise the name of the Lord.

Blessed be the name of the Lord from
this time forth and for evermore.

From the rising of the sun unto the going down
of the same the Lord's name is to be praised.

The Lord is high above all nations,
and his glory above the heavens.

—Psalm 113:1-4

Contents

Preface

In our study of the gospel we sometimes become so preoccupied with pebbles on the beach that we miss the majesty and beauty of the ocean. As an example, we need think only of something as common as birth, a miracle so much with us that we do not even pause to reverence its grandeur. Some doctrines of marvelous import and of surpassing worth are so ubiquitous, so interwoven in the texts of holy writ, that we are prone to pass over them without the reflection and appreciation worthy of their spiritual substance. These often imperceptible doctrinal seeds, when discovered and properly nourished, frequently grow into great oaks of theological understanding.

Few doctrines are more easily found but seldom noticed than that doctrine that pertains to the sacred name of Deity. Few doctrines have within them greater power to bring the children of God to a spiritual union with him than that doctrine which attests to man's origin and destiny in the family of the Gods. It nurtures the soil in which the seed of faith is planted, is as water to the tree of life, and pollinates all the doctrines of salvation. No divine message, no prophetic pronouncement, no rite or ordinance can draw the breath of spiritual life independent of the sacred name of Jesus Christ. Indeed, in his holy name is found the life and light of all things.

The topic evokes a sense of reverence, and in that spirit we as the authors have sought to increase the reader's understanding of it. This work is a brief treatment of a marvelous subject. It is a subject worthy of cultivation, one which yields the best and sweetest of fruits. To the best of our understanding, everything within the covers of this book is in harmony with the teachings of the scriptures and the words of living Apostles and prophets. Nevertheless the responsibility for what is written here is ours alone.

Acknowledgments

The doctrinal seeds for this book were planted in our hearts at the April 1985 annual conference of the Church. At that conference Elder Dallin H. Oaks captivated our attention with a penetrating discourse on what it means to take upon us the name of Christ. Subsequently we read an undelivered sermon prepared by Elder Bruce R. McConkie which he had entitled "In His Holy Name," a sermon which he had earlier planned to deliver at that very conference. Our study of the Book of Mormon caused us to reflect on this topic again and again. We have nurtured the seed and found the fruit to be most delicious.

We extend appreciation to Lauren Baum, a capable and conscientious research assistant, for her excitement with this project. We also acknowledge the encouragement of those with whom we labor in the department of Ancient Scripture at Brigham Young University, and particularly the interest of Dean Robert J. Matthews of Religious Education. As always we owe a special debt of gratitude to our wives, Shauna and Brenda, who have borne the greater burden of family responsibilities while we sought the quiet hours to work on this book.

Chapter 1

"All That Thou Doest"

> All things must be done in the
> name of Christ, whatsoever ye do in
> the Spirit.
> —D&C 46:31

W ho shall declare his generation?'' (Isaiah 53:8), Isaiah asked regarding the promised Messiah. That is, Who shall testify of his genesis? Who shall herald his roots? Who shall identify his Father? To which we answer: Those to whom the Father has manifested himself. Competence as a witness is predicated on knowledge. Those whose testimony is dependent on scriptural writ alone are second-hand witnesses; their testimony is hearsay. Establishing the truths of salvation demands more than a distant echo from the hill country of Judah; to perform baptisms requires more than the knowledge that sins were once washed away in the waters of the Jordan River.

It is one thing to read the commission the Savior gave to the meridian Twelve and quite another to have hands placed upon one's head and receive that same authority. We are left to wonder if those professing priesthood by virtue of having read the account of its conferral upon the ancients will be equally satisfied with a written account of the heavenly glories obtained by those ancients. It is of competent witness that we write. It is of the restoration of the power and authority to speak and act in the name of Christ that we testify.

The Revelation of God and the Restoration of His Authority

"And now, after the many testimonies which have been given of him, this is the testimony, last of all [meaning most recently], that we give of him: That he lives!" wrote Joseph Smith and Sidney Rigdon. "For we saw him, even on the right hand of God; and we heard the voice bearing record that he is the Only Begotten of the Father—that by him, and through him, and of him, the worlds are and were created, and the inhabitants thereof are begotten sons and daughters unto God." (D&C 76:22-23.) Such is the nature of the testimony upon which the greatest of all gospel dispensations rests. As Latter-day Saints we raise the voice of warning, the voice of those who have seen and heard, the voice of those commissioned by the lips of the Holy One, the voice of those ordained by angels from the divine presence. "Wherefore, I the Lord, knowing the calamity which should come upon the inhabitants of the earth, called upon my servant Joseph Smith, Jun., and spake unto him from heaven, and gave him commandments: and also gave commandments to others, that they should proclaim these things unto the world" (D&C 1:17-18).

"Now, what do we hear in the gospel which we have received? A voice of gladness! A voice of mercy from heaven; and a voice of truth out of the earth; glad tidings for the dead; a voice of gladness for the living and the dead; glad tidings of great joy. How beautiful upon the mountains are the feet of those that bring glad tidings of good things, and that say unto Zion: Behold, thy God reigneth! As the dews of Carmel, so shall the knowledge of God descend upon them! And again, what do we hear? Glad tidings from Cumorah! Moroni, an angel from heaven, declaring the fulfillment of the prophets—the book to be revealed," the new witness for Christ. (D&C 128:19-20.)

The voice of him that crieth in the wilderness, "Prepare ye the way of the Lord, make straight in the desert a highway for our God" (Isaiah 40:3), speaking to Joseph and Oliver saying, "In the name of Messiah I confer the Priesthood of Aaron" (D&C 13). The voice of Peter, James, and John bestowing the Holy Priesthood after the Order of the Son of God, with all its rights, keys, and powers (D&C 128:20). The voice of "divers angels, from Michael or Adam down to the present time, all declaring their dispensation, their rights, their keys, their honors, their majesty and glory, and the power of their priesthood; giving line upon line, precept upon precept; here a little, and there a little; giving us consolation by holding forth that which is to come, confirming our hope!" (D&C 128:21).

Though all who read the Bible may be edified by it, it is one thing to have read it and quite another to have been instructed by its authors and to have received authority and blessings under their hands. Who among modern divines can tell of having stood face to face with Adam, Enoch, Noah, Moses, Elijah, John the son of Zacharias, and Peter, James, and John? While religious leaders of his day spoke of a closed canon, Joseph Smith was being tutored by ancient prophets who laid their hands upon his head and conferred upon him the power, keys, and authority they held. "Joseph Smith knew the Bible, he knew its prophets, he knews its message, and he knew its central character, the Lord Jesus Christ, with whom he also stood face to face and by whom he was instructed." (Joseph Fielding McConkie, "Joseph Smith and the Poetic Writings," in Nyman and Millet, eds, *The Joseph Smith Translation: The Restoration of Plain and Precious Things*, p. 119.) He was a competent witness, one clothed in the authority of heaven. It was his right—indeed, his responsibility—to speak in the name of the Lord; he was a living Bible, a modern Moses. Thus Joseph Smith and the revelations of the Restoration become the primary source to which we turn for an understanding of the importance of taking upon us the name of Christ.

Restoring Israel to the Knowledge of Their God

As God sought anciently to make of Israel a kingdom of priests, a nation of prophets, such is his purpose in our day. The ancient gospel has been restored "that every man might speak in the name of God the Lord, even the Savior of the world," that the message of faith might go forth, that his everlasting covenant might be established, and that the fulness of the gospel might be proclaimed unto the ends of the earth. (D&C 1:20-23.) Israel is to be restored to her ancient glory; and "my people shall know my name," the Lord said, "therefore they shall know in that day that I am he that doth speak: behold, it is I" (Isaiah 52:6). To bear his name is to hear his voice, for the Lord has always spoken to those whom he professed as his own (see D&C 113:10).

There is no reason or purpose in the restoration of the kingdom of Israel, or the gathering of its scattered remnants from the ends of the earth, save it be that they are returned to the proper worship of their God and to the covenant of salvation that he made with their fathers. It is to Christ that Israel returns; it is to membership in his Church and kingdom; it is to the covenants of salvation—those sacred ordinances in which they take upon themselves his holy name and promise always to remember him, that his Spirit might always be with them. It is in his fold that they seek refuge after the long night of darkness in which they have wandered, having lost their way. The Lord has promised to gather his people even as a hen gathereth her chickens under her wings, even as many as will hearken to his voice and humble themselves before him and call upon him in mighty prayer (see D&C 29:2).

The Doctrine of the Name of Christ

What, then, are the great principles, lessons, and promised blessings associated with our taking upon us the name of Christ? Where do we begin and of what matters shall we speak?

We must speak of what it means to be his seed, to be adopted into the holy family, and to bear the sacred name of our God.

We must speak of the charge given the earthly family of our Heavenly Father to do in his name all that they do for their own salvation and for that of others.

We must speak of that doctrine whereby salvation is found in a name, of how Christ took the name of his Father, and how we are invited—or rather commanded—to take his name that we might be heirs of God and joint heirs with the Only Begotten.

We must speak of those things and places upon which he has placed his name, and of how we obtain the fulness of the blessings of his holy dwelling place.

We must speak by way of warning, carefully considering how the name of our God, the hope of our salvation, is used in vain—for surely he does not hold them guiltless that take his name in vain.

We must speak by way of testimony—identifying the doctrine of standing as witnesses not of Christ alone but also of the name of Christ, the only name by which salvation comes.

Chapter 2

The Doctrine of Sacred Names

> But now thus saith the Lord that created thee, O Jacob, and he that formed thee, O Israel, Fear not; for I have redeemed thee, I have called thee by thy name; thou art mine.
> —Isaiah 43:1

That special significance is attached in the gospel plan to names is clearly evidenced by the command of the angel of the Lord to Joseph and Mary that they bestow the proper name upon the child whose birth he foretold. "Thou shalt call his name JESUS: for he shall save his people from their sins," the angel declared (Matthew 1:21; compare Luke 1:31). *Jesus* is the Greek form of the Hebrew *Yeshua* or *Joshua*. It means "Jehovah saves" or "Jehovah is salvation." Though a common male name among the Jews, its usage in this instance was to find the full intent of its meaning. To it was added the sacred title *Christ*, meaning "anointed" or "anointed one," which is the exact equivalent in Greek for the word *Messiah*. Thus the testimony would be raised in all the world that there is salvation in no other name; "for there is none other name under heaven given among men, whereby we must be saved" (Acts 4:12).

How It Is That Salvation
Is Found in a Name

Entrance into the kingdom of heaven requires that we take upon ourselves the name of Christ. Salvation, we are told, is found in none other name (see Mosiah 5:8-10; Alma 5:38-39; D&C 18:21-25). The significance of this proclamation is worthy of careful consideration. How is it that the power of salvation is vested in a name? Be it remembered that Christ in his mortal ministry was most careful to establish the fact that he came in his "Father's name" (John 5:43), that he taught no doctrines save the doctrines of the Father (see John 7:16), that all his works were done in the name of the Father (see John 10:25), and that he sought to glorify the name of the Father in all he did (see John 12:28). Paul refers to Christ as the great Apostle of our faith (see Hebrews 3:1). Literally, the word *apostle* means "he that is sent." In the Gospel of John, Christ is quoted well over a hundred times as announcing that he was sent of his Father, and that he did nothing save that which the Father commanded him (see John 5:30). Thus the Son assumed the name and power of his Father, and through that name and by that power he extended the promise of salvation to all who would take upon themselves his (the Son's) name as he had taken upon himself the name of his Father. Such is the system of salvation.

The idea that blessings come through a name finds expression in one of society's oldest traditions. It has been the custom of fathers in all ages, and we suppose among virtually all peoples, to place their name upon their posterity. As the crown of womanhood is in granting life, so the crown of manhood is the conferring upon one's posterity the family name. Often ceremony and ritual are associated with a father placing his name, his most prized possession, upon the newborn. In the giving of a name the father declares the child to be his; he makes of him or her a rightful heir of all that he possesses, and effectually promises to love and protect his progeny, for the child is but the manifestation of his own flesh and blood. The children in return are taught to love and respect their parents and to so live as to bring honor to the name that has been given them as a sacred trust. The rebellious child can be disinherited and thus be caused to forefeit all blessings associated with bearing the family name.

Such traditions appear to reach back to man's most ancient roots. Adam was created first, then Eve was given as a help meet for him, and God "blessed them, and called their name Adam" (Moses 6:9). Thus Eve took upon herself the name of him from whom she is represented in a figurative sense as having received life, and they twain became one flesh. This perfect union that was to exist between them, represented by Eve's being created from the rib of Adam, is cited as the reason that a man was to leave his father and his mother and cleave unto his wife that they too might become one flesh as well as one name (see Genesis 2:23-24).

The giving of a name to something implies dominion, rule, or stewardship over that being named. Thus Adam, who had been commanded to subdue the earth and have dominion over all life forms upon it, was directed of the Lord to give all things a name. (See Genesis 1:28; 2:19-20.) Again, we find that after the creation of the woman it was Adam who at God's behest gave her the name Eve (see Genesis 3:20; Moses 4:26). She would bear his name, and he would rule over her (see Genesis 3:16); that is, he would protect and provide for her, and he would be her king, while she would be his queen.

Such is the order and pattern of heaven. God, the Eternal Father, placed his name upon Jesus of Nazareth, his Only Begotten in the flesh, and by so doing testified that the Galilean was his own Son, and that the love and protection of heaven would be with him. Christ, a rightful heir to the dominion, power, and glory of his Father, was entrusted to act in the divine name. In turn, the Savior invited all his earthly brothers and sisters to return to that heavenly family of which they were once a part, to take again the family name, and become heirs of the blessings associated with it.

The message is to all: "Hearken and listen to the voice of him who is from all eternity to all eternity, the Great I AM, even Jesus Christ—the light and the life of the world; a light which shineth in darkness and the darkness comprehendeth it not; the same which came in the meridian of time unto mine own, and mine own received me not; but to as many as received me, gave I power to become my sons; and even so will I give unto as many as will receive me, power to become my sons. And verily, verily, I say unto you, he that receiveth my gospel receiveth me; and he that receiveth not my gospel receiveth not me." (D&C 39:1-5.) Thus those who receive the restored gospel and join the Church have power given them to become the sons of God —meaning, of course, sons and daughters.

This sonship, however, does not come by the verbal profession of faith alone or the ritual immersion in water alone; it is obtained by continuous faith and devotion. "For as many as are led by the Spirit of God," Paul wrote, "they are the sons of God. For ye have not received the spirit of bondage again to fear; but ye have received the Spirit of adoption, whereby we cry, Abba, Father. The Spirit itself beareth witness with our spirit, that we are the children of God: and if children, then heirs; heirs of God, and joint-heirs with Christ; if so be that we suffer with him, that we may be also glorified together." (Romans 8:14-17.) The sons of God are members of his family and, hence, are joint-heirs with Christ, inheriting with him the fulness of the Father (see D&C 93:17-23). Before gaining entrance to that glorious household, they must receive the higher priesthood (see Moses 6:67-68), magnify their callings therein (see D&C 84:33), enter into the new and everlasting covenant of marriage (see D&C 131:1-4), and be obedient in all things. To such the promise is that in the world to come they shall receive the fulness of the Father (see D&C 93:19; 132:19-20) and be accounted as equal with him "in power, and in might, and in dominion" (D&C 76:95).

The whole concept of the latter-day gathering of Israel centers in the promise that Jacob's posterity, a lost and fallen people, will return to their God and once more take his name upon them. "I have called thee by thy name," the Lord says of such, "thou art mine. . . . For I am the Lord thy God, the Holy One of Israel, thy Saviour. . . . Fear not: for I am with thee: I will bring thy seed from the east, and gather thee from the west; I will say to the north, Give up; and to the south, Keep not back: bring my sons from far, and my daughters from the ends of the earth; even every one that is called by my name." (Isaiah 43:1-7.)

Those Refusing the Name of Christ

Just as we take upon ourselves the name of Christ and become the sons and daughters of God and heirs to his kingdom, so we can take upon us the name of the adversary and become heirs of the kingdom of darkness. Thus Cain through his rebellion took upon himself the name Perdition (see Moses 5:24), as will others who, like Cain, receive the fulness of gospel truth and then choose to deny it and war against it (see D&C 76:31-33).

To the supposedly religious of his day who rejected him, Christ said: "Ye are of your father the devil, and the lusts of your father ye will do. He was a murderer from the beginning, and abode not in the truth, because there is no truth in him. When he speaketh a lie, he speaketh of his own: for he is a liar, and father of it." (John 8:44.) "Remember," Abinadi said, "that he that persists in his own carnal nature, and goes on in the ways of sin and rebellion against God, remaineth in his fallen state and the devil hath all power over him. Therefore he is as though there was no redemption made, being an enemy to God" (Mosiah 16:5). In the ancient world such were called the sons of Belial (see Deuteronomy 13:13; Judges 19:22; 20:13; 1 Samuel 10:27).

The Significance of Names

Names are verbal symbols: they announce existence, herald one's reputation, and express character; they are, in some instances, a scepter of authority or even a crown of glory. Biblical names generally were descriptive of the one bearing them. They might identify position, memorialize a significant event in someone's life, express a hope entertained by those giving the name, or even represent a prophesied destiny. To "call one's name" over something signified ownership, possession, and protection—for example, of David over a city (see 2 Samuel 12:28), of seven women seeking the name of a man to take away their reproach (see Isaiah 4:1), of God over the nations (see Amos 9:12) and over Israel (see Isaiah 63:19). To "cut off the name" was the equivalent of liquidating the person (see Deuteronomy 7:24). "In modern usage, names are convenient labels by which we differentiate one thing from another, one person from another. But in the ancient world Shakespeare's question 'What's in a name?' would have been taken very seriously. For a person's self was expressed and contained in his name. Analogously, God's self, his real person, is concentrated in his name." (Anderson, "Names of God," in *Interpreter's Dictionary of the Bible,* 2:408.)

Philo referred to names as the shadow of an accompanying reality (see Bromiley, *Theological Dictionary of the New Testament,* p. 697). An act of Peter's serves as a perfect example. When he healed the lame beggar at the gate of the temple called Beautiful his words were: "Silver and gold have I none; but such as I have give I thee: In the name of Jesus Christ of Nazareth rise up and walk" (Acts 3:6). Though the miracle was performed in the name of Christ and by the power associated with that name, Peter's language clearly portrays the idea that the power and authority of the exalted name rested within him. Peter did not implore the heavens in behalf of his impotent supplicant; rather he spoke by way of command—"In the name of Jesus Christ of Nazareth rise up and walk." Such was the pattern of the meridian Apostles, and so great was the faith that they evoked in the populace that we read that the sick and afflicted were brought into the streets and laid on beds and couches, "that at the least the shadow of Peter passing by might overshadow some of them" (Acts 5:15).

After Peter and John had been threatened by the voice of the Sanhedrin, they were later freed to return to the assembly of the Saints. Peter praised the power of God, saying that "by stretching forth thine hand" they were able in the name of Jesus to heal and do all manner of signs and wonders. (See Acts 4:13-30.)

Such is the manner in which true disciples endowed with the requisite power become the extension of their Master. Thus we read that "God wrought special miracles by the hands of Paul: so that from his body were brought unto the sick handkerchiefs or aprons, and the diseases departed from them, and the evil spirits went out of them." When certain Jewish exorcists sought to use the name of Christ to cast out a devil "the evil spirit answered and said, Jesus I know, and Paul I know; but who are ye?" and then attacked those who had attempted to cast him out using a false priesthood. A spirit of reverence fell upon the Saints "and the name of the Lord Jesus was magnified." (Acts 19:11-17.)

The sacred names of Christ and of his Father do not stand alone among the Saints as names worthy of honor. Other names, though of an obviously lower stature than the designations of Deity, also are held in reverence among the household of faith. Among the chief of these would be the names of Melchizedek, after whom the greater priesthood was named; Abraham, the father of the faithful in the covenant of salvation; and Israel, the patriarch of the twelve tribes. The name Melchizedek, "being by interpretation King of righteousness" (Hebrews 7:2), attests that all who hold this holy priesthood are destined to rule as priests and kings, but that they can do so only in righteousness. The name Abraham means "father of nations," and stands as a reminder that God has promised those who enter into and prove faithful in the new and everlasting covenant of marriage that their seed will continue both in the world and out of the world, as countless as the stars and as numberless as the sand upon the seashore (see D&C 132:30-31). "Thy name," Jacob was told, "shall be called no more Jacob, but Israel: for as a prince hast thou power with God and with men, and hast prevailed" (Genesis 32:28). Jacob's new name, the name by which his descendants and eventually the righteous of all future ages would be known, was Israel, announcing that they too had prevailed with God.

That which represents the Lord carries with it a spirit that evidences its ties with the powers of heaven. There is a spirit associated with the payment of an honest tithe, keeping the Sabbath holy, studying the scriptures, bearing testimony, or teaching the gospel, that cannot be experienced in any other way. In like manner there is a mantle associated with priesthood offices and callings that is reserved for those chosen to serve in them and yet is fully evident to those who sustain them in those callings. President Spencer W. Kimball spoke of visiting places in southern Chile and in little cities in northern Argentina where people had never seen a General Authority before. People came to these meetings from long distances and at great personal expense to see an Apostle of the Lord. Reflecting on the experience, President Kimball observed: "I felt tremendously humble, like bowing my head . . . and then I recognized again that I am but a symbol to them. They did not know me. They had never seen me. They came not to see me. They came to see the apostle and their reverence and their interest was to the Church, to its leadership, to the program, and I was but a symbol, and it makes me humble indeed." (*The Teachings of Spencer W. Kimball*, p. 235.)

Conclusion

George Albert Smith, the seventh president of the Church, bore the name of his grandfather, George A. Smith. His grandfather, the youngest Apostle called in this dispensation, eventually served as a counselor to President Brigham Young. George Albert tells of a dream in which he passed to the other side of the veil, doing so with the feeling that his work in mortality was finished. The only person he met in this dream was his grandfather, who, with great earnestness, said: "I would like to know what you have done with my name."

"Everything I had ever done," President Smith said, "passed before me as though it were a flying picture on a screen—everything I had done. Quickly this vivid retrospect came down to the very time I was standing there. My whole life had passed before me. I smiled and looked at my grandfather and said:

'I have never done anything with your name of which you need be ashamed.'

"He stepped forward and took me in his arms, and as he did so, I became conscious again of my earthly surroundings. My pillow was as wet as though water had been poured on it—wet with tears of gratitude that I could answer unashamed." (Smith, *Sharing the Gospel With Others*, p. 112.) It is a law of heaven that we honor our parents and in so doing bring honor to that family of which we are a part. As the day will come when we will be required to give an accounting to them as to what we did with the name they gave us, so the day will come when we will be required to account for the manner in which we bore the name of Christ.

Indeed, names are symbols—divinely ordained teaching devices—which mirror the order of heaven and illustrate how the blessings of salvation come. We can no more save ourselves than we can give birth to ourselves. We are granted life in the name of another. We are succored and nurtured in that name. Indeed, it becomes to us the source of love, safety, protection, knowledge, and power. Thus we come to love and honor those whose name we bear, those who have freely given all they have that we might enjoy like blessings and eventually grant those same blessings to others. Such is the system of salvation: through baptism we are born into the family of Christ, and there we covenant to take and honor his name. As we do so we come to know his love and to have extended to us the blessing of heirship. All of this our Eternal Father has promised us—even the power to create others as we have been created. Such is the doctrine of sacred names.

Taking His Name Upon Us

Chapter 3

> Wherefore, all men must take upon
> them the name which is given of
> the Father, for in that name shall
> they be called at the last day.
> —D&C 18:24

There is a name that is above every name that is named, whether on earth or in heaven, save only the name of the almighty Elohim. There is a name that brings joy to the desolate heart, a name that speaks peace to the sorrowing soul. There is a name that falls in hushed and hallowed tones from the lips of Saints and angels, a name that leads true believers on both sides of the veil to glory and honor everlasting. It is the name of the one sent of God to bring salvation, the name of the one who paid an infinite price to ransom us from Satan's grasp. It is the blessed name of Jesus Christ.

Estrangement from the Family of God

The fall of Adam and Eve, though a fortunate fall and an essential step toward mortality and thus a pillar in the plan of salvation, brought about dramatic changes in the earth and all forms of life on it. The Fall introduced physical death—made inevitable the separation of man's spirit and body. It introduced spiritual death—made inevitable the separation of man from God and things of righteousness. As a result of the Fall, all mankind leave the premortal world to come forth into a fallen state, a telestial condition. "And the Lord spake unto Adam, saying: Inasmuch as thy children are conceived in sin, even so when they begin to grow up, sin conceiveth in their hearts, and they taste the bitter, that they may know to prize the good" (Moses 6:55). Those who arrive at the years of accountability become susceptible to the enticements of the flesh and the allurements of a natural state. Whenever persons succumb to the pull of the flesh they thus become natural men, enemies of God; they are "without God in the world, and they have gone contrary to the nature of God; therefore, they are in a state contrary to the nature of happiness" (Alma 41:11; see also Mosiah 3:19).

Spiritual death represents an alienation from God, in a sense a disinheritance from the royal family. Unless appropriate reconciliation with the family head is made, the blessings and the family name may be lost. That is, unless an at-one-ment is brought to pass, one loses that kind of association and sociality, that family life of which the scriptures speak—eternal life. He or she then is nameless and familyless. They are spiritual orphans and thereby alone in the world; from an eternal perspective, in the words of Malachi, they have neither root nor branch (see Malachi 4:1). In order to experience those joys and feel that warmth known only in family living, one must be reinstated in the family, literally re-deemed, or deemed worthy once again of the privileges and opportunities of being called a son or daughter of God.

The New Birth and Covenant Adoption

Deliverance from this state—redemption from spiritual death—is made available only through the labors of a God, through the majesterial ministry of one mightier than death, one upon whom justice had no claims and death had no hold. But deliverance is not a given, not something that may be had without effort and without price. In order to be released from carnality and restored to righteousness, men and women must exercise saving faith in Jesus Christ and thus receive the blessings of the Atonement: they must "put off the natural man" through Christ, must "crucify the old man of sin" and rise through their Redeemer unto a "newness of life" (see Mosiah 3:19; Romans 6:6).

Because people are not born in mortality into the family of God, because on earth man is estranged by the fall from holiness, he must be *adopted* into that family—must comply with the laws of adoption, must meet the lawful requirements. This is accomplished through subscribing to and receiving what Joseph Smith called the "articles of adoption," the first principles and ordinances of the gospel (see *Teachings of the Prophet Joseph Smith*, p. 328). "Faith, repentance, baptism and the laying on of hands," wrote Elder Orson Pratt, "are the four rules of adoption. Remission of sins, and the gift of the Holy Ghost, are the two blessings of adoption which are inseparably connected with obedience to the rules. Both the rules and the blessings of adoption are the same in all ages and dispensations of the gospel. No man or woman ever entered into the Church or kingdom of God on this earth, and became a legal citizen thereof, without complying strictly with these rules. Indeed, it is the only door or entrance into the kingdom." ("The Kingdom of God," in *Orson Pratt's Works*, p. 48.) Further, as a person receives the ordinances of salvation and thereafter enjoys the gift and influence of the Holy Ghost, he is said to have been "born again," to have risen above spiritual death unto spiritual life, to have come alive to the things of the Spirit.

As the Savior and foreordained Messiah, Jesus our Lord became the "author of eternal salvation unto all them that obey him'' (Hebrews 5:9), and the Father's gospel — the gospel of God (see Romans 1:1-3) — became his, the gospel of Jesus Christ. Christ is the father of salvation, the father of resurrection, and the father of redemption. He is also the King of kings, and spiritual adoption represents acceptance into his family kingdom. Those who have been born again become members of the family of Christ and thus take upon them the family name — they become Christians in the true sense of that word and are obligated by covenant to live by the rules and regulations of the royal family, to live a life befitting the new and sacred name they have taken.

Standards and Attributes of the Royal Family

"Family members bear the family name," Elder Bruce R. McConkie explained.

> By it they are known and called and identified; it sets them apart from all those of a different lineage and ancestry. Adopted children take upon themselves the name of their newfound parents and become in all respects as though they had been born in the family. And so it is that the children of Christ, those who are born again, those who are spiritually begotten by their new Father, take upon themselves the name of Christ. By it they are known; in it they are called; it identifies and sets them apart from all others. They are now family members, Christians in the real and true sense of the word.
>
> Do they themselves become Christs? Not in the sense that they are called upon to atone for the sins of others and make immortality and eternal life available for themselves or their fellowmen on this or any world. But they do carry his name and are obligated to bear it in decency and dignity. (*The Promised Messiah*, p. 363.)

Children will generally come to reflect the character and qualities of their parents. Those of the household of faith who remain true and faithful to their covenants—members of the Lord's Church, those who have taken upon themselves his name in the waters of baptism—come to embody and radiate the attributes of their Master.

Alma inquired of the members of the Church in his day: "And now behold, I ask of you, my brethren of the church, have ye spiritually been born of God? *Have ye received his image in your countenances?* Have ye experienced this mighty change in your hearts?" (Alma 5:14, italics added.) Those who are "in Christ" have become "new creatures" through the regenerating powers of his blood (see 2 Corinthians 5:17). Those who have been born again evidence the freshness and innocence of youth but the steadiness of spiritual maturity—they walk in the light as their Master is in the light, and they show forth those fruits of faith, the fruits of the Spirit, the attributes of him whose they are. "The fruit of the Spirit," wrote Paul, "is love, joy, peace, longsuffering, gentleness, goodness, faith, meekness, temperance." (Galatians 5:22-23.)

Those who have been born again seek earnestly to overcome the world, to cast off carnality and live as becometh Saints. They seek to be true to the family, to bring honor to their Father's name. They seek to emulate and imitate their Lord and Exemplar, he who overcame all things. "Ye shall be even as I am," Christ exhorted the Nephites, "and I am even as the Father; and the Father and I are one" (3 Nephi 28:10; see also 27:27). "Whosoever is born of God," John taught, "doth not continue in sin; for the Spirit of God remaineth in him; and he cannot continue in sin, because he is born of God, having received that holy Spirit of promise" (JST, 1 John 3:9). Truly the members of the body of Christ "manifest before the church, and also before the elders, by a godly walk and conversation, that they are worthy of it, that there may be works and faith agreeable to the holy scriptures—walking in holiness before the Lord" (D&C 20:69).

Joint Heirs with Christ: Children of God the Father

It was never intended that men and women remain children forever, even children of Jesus Christ. After a person has received the appropriate ordinances and made the appropriate covenants; after he has chosen to forsake evil, has begun to have dross and iniquity burned out of his soul as though by fire, has become alive to the things of the Spirit and thus been born again; after he has taken the name of Christ and become his son by covenant—after these developments he may begin to mature spiritually, receive further covenants and ordinances, and receive even greater endowments of the Holy Ghost. Elder Bruce R. McConkie has described this process as follows:

> As men pursue the goal of eternal life, they first enter in at the gate of repentance and baptism, thereby taking upon themselves the name of Christ. They then gain power to become his sons and daughters, to be adopted into his family, to be brethren and sisters in his kingdom. Baptism standing alone does not transform them into family members, but it opens the door to such a blessed relationship; and if men so live as to obtain the Spirit and are in fact born again then they become members of the Holy Family.
>
> Then, if they press forward with a steadfastness in Christ, keeping the commandments and living by every word that proceedeth forth from the mouth of God, they qualify for *celestial marriage,* and *this gives them power to become the sons of God, meaning the Father. They thus become joint heirs with Christ who is his natural heir. Those who are sons of God in this sense are the ones who become gods in the world to come.* (D&C 76:54-60.) They have exaltation and godhood because the family unit continues in eternity. (D&C 132:19-24.) (*Doctrinal New Testament Commentary,* 2:474, italics added.)

"For as many as are led by the Spirit of God," Paul wrote, *"they are the sons of God.* For ye have not received the spirit of bondage again to fear; but ye have received the Spirit of adoption, whereby we cry, Abba, Father. The Spirit itself beareth witness with our spirit, that *we are the children of God:* and if children, then heirs; *heirs of God, and joint heirs with Christ;* if so be that we suffer with him, that we may be also glorified together. For I reckon that the sufferings of this present time are not worthy to be compared with the glory which shall be revealed in us." (Romans 8:14-18, italics added.) Of such persons—of those who qualify to be joint heirs, co-inheritors with Christ to all that the Father has—the revelations affirm: "They are they who are the church of the Firstborn. They are they into whose hands the Father has given all things." And further, "as it is written, *they are gods, even the sons of God."* (D&C 76:54-55, 58, italics added; compare 76:24; 132:20.)

Conclusion

As God has placed his name upon his blessed Son, so has that Son placed his holy name upon those who come into his Church, join his family, and bear his name with dignity and fidelity and devotion. The plan of salvation thus provides the means whereby estranged and fallen men and women may rise above the world, escape the alienation of spiritual orphanage, and be adopted by covenant and thereafter sealed into the royal family of God our Father. The promise of our Lord and Master is ever before us: "And blessed is he that is found faithful unto my name at the last day, for he shall be lifted up to dwell in the kingdom prepared for him from the foundation of the world. And behold it is I that hath spoken it. Amen." (Ether 4:19.)

Chapter 4

His Name Through the Ages

> Wherefore, thou shalt do all that
> thou doest in the name of the Son,
> and thou shalt repent and call upon
> God in the name of the Son forevermore.
> —Moses 5:8

There is but one gospel, one plan of salvation, one name by which the blessings of heaven are obtained. Whenever that gospel has been enjoyed by the children of men, whenever the ordinances of salvation have been available to them, whenever sins have been remitted, miracles wrought, revelations vouchsafed, and the promises of eternity granted—whenever these blessings have been given to man the holy name of Christ the Lord has been made known and has been held in sacred remembrance by the faithful. It could not be otherwise, for there is but one name under heaven whereby salvation comes. The declaration by the angel to father Adam echoes through all ages: "Thou shalt do all that thou doest in the name of the Son, and thou shalt repent and call upon God in the name of the Son forevermore" (Moses 5:8).

The Ancient Saints and the Name of Christ

The light of modern revelation makes plain a vital verity: that Christian prophets have declared Christian doc-

trine and administered Christian ordinances since the days
of Eden; that the atonement of Christ has been in effect
since creation's dawn; that Jehovah is the "Lamb slain
from the foundation of the world" (Revelation 13:8; compare Moses 7:47); and thus that men have called upon the
sacred name of Jesus Christ from the beginning of time.
God "called upon our father Adam by his own voice, saying: I am God; I made the world, and men before they
were in the flesh. And he also said unto him: If thou wilt
turn unto me, and hearken unto my voice, and believe,
and repent of all thy transgressions, and be baptized, even
in water, in the name of mine Only Begotten Son, who is
full of grace and truth, which is Jesus Christ, *the only
name which shall be given under heaven, whereby salvation shall come unto the children of men,* ye shall receive
the gift of the Holy Ghost, asking all things in his name,
and whatsoever ye shall ask, it shall be given you."
(Moses 6:51-52, italics added.)

One of the "plain and precious truths" restored
through the Book of Mormon and other modern revelations
is the assurance that the ancient Saints knew their God;
that they knew they were to call upon the Father in the
name of the Son; and that they knew that salvation was to
be had in the holy name of Jehovah-Christ and in none
other. If our present Old Testament had come down to us
in the same condition as the brass plates of Laban, it would
read as plainly on this matter as the Book of Mormon does
(see 1 Nephi 13:23). But having what we have—the witness of the Book of Mormon prophets and the singular in-
sights delivered by revelation through Joseph Smith—we
are able to recognize the doctrine of the sacred name in the
ancient writings.

Before we cite a few of the numerous passages from the
Old Testament that illustrate these principles, the reader
should have clearly in mind that nearly all the passages of
scripture which speak of men and women as the sons and
daughters of God refer, not to our birth in premortal exis-

tence but rather to the fact that through our existing faith in Jehovah-Christ he becomes our Father—that is, we become his children by adoption (see Bruce R. McConkie, *The Promised Messiah,* pp. 351-52). Indeed, the doctrine of adoption—taught so plainly by the Apostle Paul (see Romans 8; Galatians 3-4)—was not unique to first-century Christianity but was common to the understanding of the Saints of God in all previous ages.

Aaron, the brother of Moses, was instructed by Jehovah to pronounce the following blessing upon the children of Israel: "The Lord bless thee, and keep thee: the Lord make his face shine upon thee, and be gracious unto thee: the Lord lift up his countenance upon thee, and give thee peace. *And they* [Aaron and his sons] *shall put my name upon the children of Israel; and I will bless them.*" (Numbers 6:23-27, italics added.) "The Lord shall establish thee an holy people unto himself," Moses wrote, "as he hath sworn unto thee, if thou shalt keep the commandments of the Lord thy God, and walk in his ways. And all people of the earth shall see that *thou art called by the name of the Lord* [Jehovah]; and they shall be afraid of thee." (Deuteronomy 28:9-10, italics added.) Centuries later Jehovah spoke through Solomon: "If my people, *which are called by my name,* shall humble themselves, and pray, and seek my face, and turn from their wicked ways; then will I hear from heaven, and will forgive their sin, and will heal their land" (2 Chronicles 7:14, italics added; compare Jeremiah 14:9).

Through Hosea the prophet, Jehovah prophesied of the ultimate triumph of the house of Israel. "The number of the children of Israel," he said, "shall be as the sand of the sea, which cannot be measured nor numbered; and it shall come to pass, that in the place where it was said unto them, Ye are not my people, there [that is, in a future day] it shall be said unto them, *Ye are the sons of the living God*" (Hosea 1:10, italics added). One of the most eloquent and touching prophetic utterances concerning the gathering of Israel and Jehovah's tender regard toward his covenant people was recorded by Isaiah.

> Thus saith the Lord that created thee, O Jacob, and he that formed thee, O Israel, Fear not: for I have redeemed thee, I have called thee by thy name; thou art mine.
>
> When thou passest through the waters, I will be with thee; and through the rivers, they shall not overflow thee: when thou walkest through the fire, thou shalt not be burned; neither shall the flame kindle upon thee.
>
> For I am the Lord thy God, the Holy One of Israel, thy Saviour: I gave Egypt for thy ransom, Ethiopia and Seba for thee.
>
> Since thou wast precious in my sight, thou hast been honourable, and I have loved thee: therefore will I give men for thee, and people for thy life.
>
> Fear not: for I am with thee: I will bring thy seed from the east, and gather thee from the west;
>
> I will say to the north, Give up; and to the south, Keep not back: *bring my sons from far, and my daughters from the ends of the earth;*
>
> *Even every one that is called by my name:* for I have created him for my glory, I have formed him; yea, I have made him. (Isaiah 43:1-7, italics added.)

The pleading cry of Israel to her God is one of appreciation, one of gratitude for his infinite patience and love. "Doubtless *thou art our father*," Israel exults, "though Abraham be ignorant of us, and Israel acknowledge us not: *thou, O Lord, art our father, our redeemer;* thy name is from everlasting" (Isaiah 63:16, italics added; compare 64:8).

The Sacred Name: Hallowed or Unspeakable?

One of the most serious doctrinal misunderstandings in the Judeo-Christian world has arisen over a biblical mistranslation. According to present translations of our Old

Testament, Jehovah remarked to Moses: "I am the Lord: and I appeared unto Abraham, unto Isaac, and unto Jacob, by the name of God Almighty, but by my name JEHOVAH was I not known to them" (Exodus 6:2-3). From this error of transcription or translation has been perpetuated the strange notion that the name of Jehovah was not revealed until Sinai. The Joseph Smith Translation of this passage corrects the text and brings the words of the Lord into harmony with what our other scriptures teach about the holy name being known from the beginning: "I appeared unto Abraham, unto Isaac, and unto Jacob. I am the Lord God Almighty; the Lord JEHOVAH. And *was not my name known unto them?"* (JST, Exodus 6:3, italics added.)

When the Lord called Moses to deliver Israel from Egyptian bondage, Moses responded: "Who am I, that I should go unto Pharaoh, and that I should bring forth the children of Israel out of Egypt?" (Exodus 3:11.) Both Enoch, centuries before Moses, and Jeremiah, centuries after (Moses 6:31; Jeremiah 1:6), manifested great concern over their inadequacies when called to the work of the Lord. The heavens, nevertheless, do compensate for those who will be taught and will allow the powers of the Spirit to work a mighty change. The Lord assured Moses that He would be with him and would give to him whatever strengths or powers would be needed to accomplish an otherwise impossible task, and that Moses would yet bring the whole house of Israel to worship the Lord on that mount.

Feeling inadequate, Moses sought credentials: "When I come unto the children of Israel, and shall say unto them, The God of your fathers hath sent me unto you; and they shall say to me, What is his name? what shall I say unto them?" Apparently Moses felt he needed to know the personal name of the God of the fathers in order to demonstrate to the leaders of Israel that he had indeed been in the presence of Deity. Honoring the request, the Lord said: "I

AM THAT I AM: and he said, Thus shalt thou say unto the children of Israel, I AM hath sent me unto you." (Exodus 3:13-14.)

The Hebrew expression *ĕhyeh ăsher ĕhyeh*, rendered "I AM THAT I AM" in the King James translation, is a penetrating statement, and one which has received much attention over the centuries. The word *ĕhyeh* is a conjugation of the verb *hayah*, "to be," and is thus closely related to the concept of being. The personal name of the Lord in Hebrew is given in transliteration by the four letters (called tetragrammaton) YHWH or JHVH and was probably pronounced Yahweh, also a conjugation of the verb "to be." There are many possible meanings or explanations for the phrase: "I AM THAT I AM"; "I AM WHO I AM"; "I WILL BE WHOM I WILL BE." A number of Hebrew scholars are agreed that the expression represents what is known as a Hiphil construction, a causative form of the verb, in which case, in short, the Lord's words would mean "I CAUSE TO BE" or "I CAUSE TO EXIST." "In the name Jehovah or I AM, God manifests himself as a personal living being who labors in behalf of Israel and who will fulfil the promises made to the fathers. All of this conveys the idea of an unchanging, ever-living God, who through all generations is true to his word." (Joseph Fielding McConkie, *Gospel Symbolism*, p. 177.) His name manifests the verity of his nature.

We know the tetragrammaton YHWH in the anglicized form, JEHOVAH, a word that is written out in full only four times in the King James Bible (Exodus 6:3; Psalm 83:18; Isaiah 12:2; 26:4). It would seem that the intent to avoid the too frequent repetition of the name of Deity by the ancient Saints (see D&C 107:3-4)—as well as the commandment to avoid taking the name of the Lord in vain (see Exodus 20:7)—was adulterated by many over the centuries until, by the time of the Savior in the meridian of time, the Jews had come to believe it blasphemous even to speak the personal name of the God of the fathers. Their excessive zeal and misplaced reverence led to misunderstanding. Thus Jesus was attacked and almost stoned because he declared his divine sonship in these words: "Before Abraham was, I AM," or, stated in another way, "Before Abraham was I, Jehovah." (John 8:58-59.) In announcing himself as the great I AM, Jesus thus committed a double sin in the minds of the Jewish leaders of that day: he spoke the unspeakable and he declared himself the Son of Man. The translators of the King James Version, presumably desiring to hallow the sacred name, substituted "the LORD" (with capital letters) for YHWH in the Old Testament in all but the four cases mentioned above.

The revelations of the Restoration affirm, as Jesus declared prior to the agonies of Gethsemane, that it is life eternal to know God, and Jesus Christ whom he sent (see John 17:3). That Christ is to be known as the great I AM, that he is indeed the Jehovah of the Old Testament, and that he is to be known—both in heaven and on earth, by angels as well as mortals—and his name is to be spoken with appropriate reverence, is attested in modern revelation. "Thus saith the Lord your God," came the word of the Lord to Joseph Smith, "even Jesus Christ, the Great I AM, Alpha and Omega, the beginning and the end, the same which looked upon the wide expanse of eternity, and all the seraphic hosts of heaven, before the world was made" (D&C 38:1; compare 39:1). Jehovah, the first and the last, declared himself in our day to be "he who liveth, . . . he who was slain," even he who is our advocate with the Father (see D&C 110:4).

The Nephites and the Name of Christ

Setting aside the fear of being repetitious—for the scriptures themselves are marvelously repetitive on the matter of taking the name of Christ through the new birth; indeed this doctrine appears to be the burden of scripture—we will briefly illustrate the simplicity and consistency with which these verities are presented in the Nephite record, and how they will yet be found when the biblical record is restored to its pristine purity.

The Lehite colony took with them to the New World the plates of brass, an ancient scriptural record more extensive than our present Old Testament. In addition, their leaders, Lehi and Nephi, enjoyed frequent communion with the heavens even with Jehovah, the God of Abraham, Isaac, and Jacob. They had the Melchizedek Priesthood and the fulness of the gospel. The Nephite prophets taught the doctrines of salvation with a clarity unmatched in other scripture, particularly the necessity for a spiritual rebirth for all men and women who desired to become the sons and daughters of Christ. Thus it was that Nephi affirmed by oath and testimony the central role of Jesus the Messiah:

> For according to the words of the prophets, the Messiah cometh in six hundred years from the time that my father left Jerusalem; and according to the words of the prophets, and also the word of the angel of God, his name shall be Jesus Christ, the Son of God.
>
> And now, my brethren, I have spoken plainly that ye cannot err. And *as the Lord God liveth* that brought Israel up out of the land of Egypt, . . . *there is none other name given under heaven save it be this Jesus Christ,* of which I have spoken, *whereby man can be saved.* (2 Nephi 25:19-20, italics added; compare Mosiah 3:17.)

Just prior to his death, the noble King Benjamin called his people together to announce his retirement, to give an accounting of his years as king, and to announce his son Mosiah as his successor. "And moreover," he said, *"I shall give this people a name,* that thereby they may be distinguished above all the people which the Lord God hath brought out of the land of Jerusalem; and this I do because they have been a diligent people in keeping the commandments of the Lord. And I give unto them a name that never shall be blotted out, except it be through transgression." (Mosiah 1:11-12, italics added.)

Then Benjamin proceeded to deliver one of the greatest sermons of all time, a powerful utterance which evidences his nobility of soul and prophetic stature. Much of what he spoke he had learned from an angel of God. Among other things, Benjamin spoke of the necessity for service to our fellow beings as a means of serving God; of the constant need for the enlivening powers of God in our lives; of the coming of the Lord Omnipotent to earth to take a tabernacle of clay; of the necessity of putting off the natural man and becoming a Saint through the atonement of Christ the Lord; and of the importance of seeing to the needs of others as an integral step in retaining a remission of sins from day to day (see Mosiah 2-4).

The power of the occasion was such that the congregation "all cried with one voice, saying: . . . we believe all the words which thou hast spoken unto us; and also, we know of their surety and truth, because of the Spirit of the Lord Omnipotent, which has wrought a mighty change in us, or in our hearts, that we have no more disposition to do evil, but to do good continually." They further expressed their desire to renew the covenant which they had no doubt made earlier in their lives to do the will of God and to keep all of his commandments. King Benjamin, like any gospel preacher who serves as an instrument in the hands of the Lord, was thrilled with their response. "Ye have spoken the words that I desired," he said; "and the covenant which ye have made is a righteous covenant." He continued:

> And now, because of the covenant which ye have made ye shall be called the children of Christ, his sons, and his daughters; for behold, this day he hath spiritually begotten you; for ye say that your hearts are changed through faith on his name; therefore, ye are born of him and have become his sons and his daughters.
>
> And under this head ye are made free, and there is no other head whereby ye can be made free. There is no other name given whereby salvation cometh; therefore, I would that ye should take upon you the name of Christ,

all you that have entered into the covenant with God that ye should be obedient unto the end of your lives.

And it shall come to pass that whosoever doeth this shall be found at the right hand of God, for he shall know the name by which he is called; for he shall be called by the name of Christ.

And now it shall come to pass, that whosoever shall not take upon him the name of Christ must be called by some other name; therefore, he findeth himself on the left hand of God.

And I would that ye should remember also, that this is the name that I said I should give unto you that never should be blotted out, except it be through transgression; therefore, take heed that ye do not transgress, that the name be not blotted out of your hearts. (Mosiah 5:1-11, italics added.)

In teaching the doctrine of the condescension of God, Abinadi quoted to the priests of Noah what we know as Isaiah 53, the greatest messianic prophecy in our present Old Testament. In speaking of the Suffering Servant, Abinadi (quoting Isaiah) explained that "when thou [the Father] shalt make his [Christ's] soul an offering for sin he [Christ] shall see his seed" (Mosiah 14:10). Without the inspired prophetic commentary of Abinadi in the next chapter—and the confirming witness in other scriptures of the Restoration—we would be at a loss as to the meaning of these words. Abinadi explained that "whosoever has heard the words of the prophets, . . . all those who have hearkened unto their words, and believed that the Lord would redeem his people, and have looked forward to that day for a remission of their sins, I say unto you, that these are his seed, or they are the heirs of the kingdom of God." Continuing, Abinadi taught that "the prophets, every one that has opened his mouth to prophesy, that has not fallen into transgression, . . . they are his seed." (Mosiah 15:11, 13.)

In short, Abinadi helps us to understand that once the Lord of Life had shed his atoning blood in Gethsemane and on Calvary, once he had passed through the veil of death, he entered the world of spirits. There he was greeted by his seed—"an innumerable company of the spirits of the just" (D&C 138:12)—the righteous dead from the days of Adam until the meridian of time. There he taught his gospel and organized his righteous missionary forces and commissioned them to bridge the gulf between paradise and hell and thus carry the message of the gospel to those who were in darkness (see D&C 138:29-31, 37).

The conversion of Alma the Younger was a significant turning point in the Book of Mormon story. Few persons in history would make such a remarkable turnabout in life; few persons would thereafter make a more dramatic difference in the spread of the message of Christianity. Having been struck down by an angel and having spent three long days in introspection and suffering and repentance, Alma emerged from the "sleep of death" and uttered the following words: "I have repented of my sins, and have been redeemed of the Lord; behold I am born of the Spirit. And the Lord said unto me, Marvel not that all mankind, yea, men and women, all nations, kindreds, tongues and people, must be born again; yea, born of God, changed from their carnal and fallen state, to a state of righteousness, being redeemed of God, becoming his sons and daughters; and thus they become new creatures; and unless they do this, they can in nowise inherit the kingdom of God." (Mosiah 27:24-26.)

That same Alma later preached to the people of Zarahemla of the absolute necessity of being born again, of becoming new creatures, and of taking upon them the holy name of Jesus Christ. "I say unto you, that the good shepherd doth call you," he said; "yea, and in his own name he doth call you, which is the name of Christ; and if ye will not hearken unto the voice of the good shepherd, to the

name by which ye are called, behold, ye are not the sheep
of the good shepherd'' (Alma 5:38).

The Name of Christ in Modern Revelation

Among the most salient truths revealed to Joseph
Smith was the absolute necessity of spiritual rebirth, for
taking the name of Christ through entering the Church and
kingdom of God. In a revelation given to Oliver Cowdery
and David Whitmer almost a year before the Restored
Church was organized, the Lord declared: ''Take upon
you the name of Christ, and speak the truth in soberness.
. . . Behold, Jesus Christ is the name which is given of the
Father, and there is none other name given whereby man
can be saved.'' (D&C 18:21, 23.) In a revelation given
through the Prophet for his wife, the Savior reaffirmed
what the prophets and Apostles of old had declared:
''Hearken unto the voice of the Lord your God, while I
speak unto you, Emma Smith, my daughter; for verily I
say unto you, *all those who receive my gospel are sons
and daughters in my kingdom*'' (D&C 25:1, italics added;
compare 34:1-3). To James Covill the Master likewise
spoke: ''Hearken and listen,'' he said, ''to the voice of him
who is from all eternity to all eternity, the Great I AM,
even Jesus Christ—the light and the life of the world; a
light which shineth in darkness and the darkness comprehendeth it not; the same which came in the meridian of
time unto mine own, and mine own received me not; but *to
as many as received me, gave I power to become my sons;*
and even so will I give unto as many as will receive me,
power to become my sons'' (D&C 39:1-4, italics added).

Conclusion

Because of that which has been delivered to us through
Joseph Smith, we become privy to doctrines known to but
few in the religious world—that men and women have

called upon the Father in the name of the Son through all generations of time; that men and women have forsaken their sins and been renewed through the atoning blood of Him who is our advocate with the Father; that legions of earth's inhabitants have taken the name of Christ and become his by adoption. These truths affirm that the Saints of all ages are of one family, professing one faith, bearing one and the same name, and obtaining salvation in one and the same manner.

Acting in
His Name

Chapter 5

> Wherefore, as ye are agents,
> ye are on the Lord's errand; and
> whatsoever ye do according to the will
> of the Lord is the Lord's business.
> —D&C 64:29

We are the servants of the Lord, who is our Master, and he has commanded us to labor in his fields—plowing, sowing, cultivating, and harvesting. That is, we are the *agents* of the Lord, who is our *eternal principal,* and he has empowered us to represent him and do the things he would do if he were personally present. When we do all things in his name in righteousness, it means that we put ourselves in his place and stead, that we think and speak and act as he would in the same situation. It means we live our lives as though we were the one whose blessed name we bear. Our acts become his acts—they are done in his name.

Speaking in His Name

As we all know, Jesus went forth in the power of the Spirit preaching the gospel of the kingdom in all the cities and towns of Judea and Galilee. He called upon all the people to repent and believe the gospel and be saved. When our Lord preached he spoke as one having authority. "Moses and the ancient prophets told you to do such and such, but I say unto you, do thus and so." And we do not question his right so to do, for as Jehovah of the Old Testament he had given the Law, and now as Jesus Christ of the New Testament he fulfilled that Law.

Christ's servants preach in his name. They have no doctrine of their own; they proclaim his doctrine. Their word is his word and is sent in his name as though he had spoken it. Those commissioned by him are to preach his gospel by the Comforter, and whatever they speak by the power of the Holy Ghost is scripture. It is the will of the Lord, the mind of the Lord, the voice of the Lord, "and the power of God unto salvation" (D&C 68:3-4). Faithful Saints have "the mind of Christ" (1 Corinthians 2:16). They think what he thinks, believe what he believes, desire what he desires, and thus speak what he would speak. The message is his! When an inspired person, as guided by the Spirit, preaches a doctrine or gives counsel to his fellowmen and concludes the message in the name of the Lord Jesus Christ, the message is not of man but of the Lord. The messenger must always be true to the message: he is but the agent acting in behalf of his principal.

It is an awesome responsibility to speak in the name of the Lord (see *History of the Church*, 1:226). In addressing a group of gospel teachers, Elder Bruce R. McConkie said: "I often think as I go around the Church and preach in various meetings that it just does not make a snap of the fingers difference to me what I am talking about. I do not care what I talk about. All I am concerned with is getting in tune with the Spirit and expressing the thoughts, in the best language and way that I can, that are implanted there by the power of the Spirit. The Lord knows what a congregation needs to hear, and he has provided a means to give that revelation to every preacher and every teacher." ("The Foolishness of Teaching," p. 8.) The messenger of salvation will, as Alma said, "declare the word with truth and soberness" (Alma 42:31). That is, he will be faithful to the message he has been commissioned to bear.

Perhaps the most frequent illustration of what is called "the gift of tongues" is the manner in which hundreds of thousands of the Lord's Saints—every day of the year—speak as they are moved upon by the power of the Holy Ghost. Nephi taught that if one follows the example of his Savior—by being obedient to the commandment to be baptized by water as a sincere act of covenant—"then shall [he] receive the Holy Ghost; yea, then cometh the baptism of fire and of the Holy Ghost; and *then can* [he] *speak with the tongue of angels,* and shout praises unto the Holy One of Israel" (2 Nephi 31:13, italics added). Later Nephi explained:

> And now, behold, my beloved brethren, I suppose that ye ponder somewhat in your hearts concerning that which ye should do after ye have entered in by the way. But, behold, why do ye ponder these things in your hearts?
>
> Do ye not remember that I said unto you that *after ye had received the Holy Ghost ye could speak with the tongue of angels?* And now, *how could ye speak with the tongue of angels save it were by the Holy Ghost?*
>
> *Angels speak by the power of the Holy Ghost; wherefore, they speak the words of Christ.* Wherefore, I said unto you, feast upon the words of Christ; for behold, the words of Christ will tell you all things what ye should do. (2 Nephi 32:1-3, italics added.)

This is the Lord's work we are engaged in, and he is intimately involved in it. It is his Church to which we belong, his gospel which is administered by the Church, and his doctrines which we preach. Those who properly prepare to represent him—who live worthy of the guiding and sustaining influence of his Spirit—these are given his words to· speak. When so moved upon, they speak with the tongue of angels, they speak the words of Christ—they say, as the angels would, what he would want said.

One of the Brethren at a general conference of the Church observed: "If the Lord himself had chosen to come down, open the conference, and address the Saints, what message would he have delivered? If he had elected and chosen to come and speak at this session, what word would he have given us for our blessing and benefit and salvation? . . . I had it impressed upon me, when President Lee opened the conference yesterday, and again when President Romney bore the persuasive and powerful and true witness that has just come from his lips, that if the Lord himself were here, these statements which came from them are the very things that he would say at this time." (Bruce R. McConkie, in Conference Report, October 1973, p. 54.) And what is true of the leadership of the Church is equally true for the members as a whole; the Apostles and prophets are the examples, the models, the pattern of what all of the Saints of the Most High should be and do. Indeed, the everlasting gospel has been restored in our day "that every man might speak in the name of God the Lord, even the Savior of the world." And as the Lord has said of that word, "whether [it is spoken] by mine own voice or by the voice of my servants, it is the same." (D&C 1:20, 38.)

Divine Investiture of Authority

As we have observed, the Eternal Father has placed his name upon the Son (see John 5:43; 10:25). Thus, in using his Father's name, the words and acts of Jesus became and were those of his Father. There are numerous passages in scripture in which Jesus, who is the Lord Jehovah, speaks in behalf of his Father, using the very words of his Father, in the first person as though he were the Almighty Elohim. His doing so is an illustration of speaking by *divine investiture of authority.*

All direct revelation from Deity since the fall of Adam has been given by and through Jesus Christ, who is Jehovah of the Old Testament. Since that time, whenever the Father has appeared to man, he has introduced and borne witness of his Son. (See JST, John 1:19; Joseph Fielding

Smith, *Doctrines of Salvation,* 1:27.) Thus it is that the
God who has revealed himself since the expulsion from
Eden has been Jehovah-Christ, and the resultant words of
scripture—though they frequently contain the very language of Elohim the Father—are spoken through Jehovah,
who is Christ our Lord.

One of the classic illustrations of this principle is contained in a vision given to Moses, containing the "words of
God, which he spake unto Moses at a time when Moses
was caught up into an exceedingly high mountain." Having introduced himself as the Lord God Almighty, an endless being "without beginning of days or end of years,"
Jehovah spoke: "And I have a work for thee, Moses, my
son; and *thou art in the similitude of mine Only Begotten;
and mine Only Begotten is and shall be the Savior,* for he
is full of grace and truth" (Moses 1:1, 3, 6, italics added).
As we know clearly from other scriptural sources, Jehovah
is the God who revealed himself to Moses and the ancients
(JST, Exodus 6:3; 3 Nephi 15:5). And yet on this occasion
he speaks in the first person, using the language of his
Father (see *The Promised Messiah,* p. 443; *Messages of
the First Presidency,* 4:269-71).

It is not uncommon in some sections in the Doctrine
and Covenants to find the Lord Jesus speaking as both the
Father and the Son in the same revelation. For example, in
section 29, we read in the opening verse: "Listen to the
voice of Jesus Christ, your Redeemer, the Great I AM,
whose arm of mercy hath atoned for your sins." Yet later
in the same section we read: "I, the Lord God, gave unto
Adam and unto his seed, that they should not die as to the
temporal death, until I, the Lord God, should send forth
angels to declare unto them repentance and redemption,
through faith on the name of mine Only Begotten Son"
(D&C 29:42, italics added).

In section 49 we see the same principle in operation,
this time in reverse order. Verse 5 begins with: "Thus
saith the Lord; for I am God, and have sent mine Only Be-

gotten Son into the world for the redemption of the world.'' And yet the revelation ends as follows: ''Behold, *I am Jesus Christ,* and I come quickly'' (D&C 49:28, italics added).

Why would the person speaking change in the same revelation? We answer: What better way is there to establish firmly in the minds of the Saints that the words of Jehovah are the very same words as those of Elohim; that these two glorious beings have the same mind and thus the same thoughts; that they are totally and completely one? In this way the Savior establishes that he acts in the full authority of his Father. In like manner, the Holy Ghost, being one with Christ, is empowered to speak the words of Christ and the Father (see Moses 5:9). And as we have seen, angels similarly speak in behalf of their Master (see 2 Nephi 32:3; Revelation 22:8-13).

Men and women who have been ordained or set apart to teach the truths of salvation—who have been commissioned to represent him whose they are and proclaim the truths of his everlasting gospel—likewise may speak by divine investiture of authority. They do not necessarily declare, ''Thus saith the Lord.'' It is not necessary that they speak in the first person for the Father or for Jesus Christ the Son. They do stand, however, as representatives and agents of their Master and as such are entitled to the quiet but persuasive whisperings of the Holy Spirit, which, when they receive it, empowers and authorizes and justifies their utterances. God honors his servants. He vindicates the words of his chosen vessels.

Enoch, a young but spiritually mature oracle of God, was troubled because of his difficulty with speaking. ''And the Lord said unto Enoch: Go forth and do as I have commanded thee. . . . *Open thy mouth, and it shall be filled, and I will give thee utterance,* for all flesh is in my hands, and I will do as seemeth me good.'' Jehovah then added these powerful and prophetic words: ''Behold *my Spirit is upon you, wherefore all thy words will I justify;*

and the mountains shall flee before you, and the rivers
shall turn from their course; and thou shalt abide in me,
and I in you; therefore walk with me. (Moses 6:32-34, italics added.) Similarly, the Lord blessed Moses, saying:
"Thou shalt be made stronger than many waters; for they
shall obey thy command *as if thou wert God*" (Moses
1:25, italics added).

His Name Is His Authority

In yet another sense, to take upon oneself the name of
Christ is to receive his authority or power. "Behold," the
Lord said to Abraham, "I will lead thee by my hand, and I
will take thee, to put upon thee my name, even the Priesthood of thy father, and my power shall be over thee"
(Abraham 1:18). In the meridian of time the disciples of
the Lord came to understand clearly the power of the name
or authority of their Master. Luke records that the seventy
returned from their missionary labors, saying, "Lord,
even the devils are subject unto us through thy name"
(Luke 10:17).

After the resurrection of Christ, Peter and John en-
countered a lame man near the Gate Beautiful at the
temple. "Lame from his mother's womb," this man was
brought daily to a spot where he could plead for alms.
"And Peter, fastening his eyes upon him, with John, said,
Look on us. And he gave heed unto them, expecting to receive something of them." And then came the unforgetta-
ble command from the chief Apostle: "Silver and gold
have I none; but such as I have give I thee: In the name of
Jesus Christ of Nazareth rise up and walk. And [Peter]
took him by the right hand, and lifted him up: and imme-
diately his feet and ankle bones received strength. And he
leaping up stood, and walked, and entered with them into
the temple, walking, and leaping, and praising God."
(Acts 3:1-8.) Peter and John were the servants of the Lord;
they acted for him and on his behalf; they did what he

would have done had he been present. They acted in his name. Peter, be it remembered, did not pray to the Lord and ask him to heal the lame beggar. Rather, in his capacity as an agent, having authority to act in his principal's place and stead, he commanded that an impotent body be made whole. And it was so.

Peter and John were brought before the Sanhedrin for questioning after his miracle. "And when [the council] had set them in the midst, they asked, *By what power, or by what name*, have ye done this?" [The leaders of the Jews thereby equated power and name as one and the same.] Then Peter, filled with the Holy Ghost, said unto them, "Ye rulers of the people, and elders of Israel, if we this day be examined of the good deed done to the impotent man, by what means he is made whole; be it known unto you all, and to all the people of Israel, that *by the name of Jesus Christ of Nazareth*, whom ye crucified, whom God raised from the dead, *even by him doth this man stand here before you whole*." Peter then uttered the same truth uttered by prophets from the days of Adam (see Moses 6:52; 2 Nephi 25:20; Mosiah 3:17), that "there is none other name under heaven given among men, whereby we must be saved." (Acts 4:7-12, italics added.)

Certain ordinances are essential to salvation. Unless and until they are received, no man can inherit the riches of eternity. Without baptism there is no salvation; without eternal marriage there is no eternal life; without the holy priesthood men cannot rule and reign as kings and priests in the household of faith forever. That Jesus performed ordinances is well known. He baptized, conferred the Holy Ghost, administered the sacrament, ordained to priestly offices—all in the power and authority of his divine sonship. But he is not available to do these things for each individual, so he empowers others to act in his name—he extends an investiture of authority, if you will—to ensure that all have the privilege of receiving those powers and rites which enable us to become even as he is. To be valid,

the ordinances must be performed by him or by his word—
meaning, by his servants who act in his holy name. Thus
the meridian Saints rejoiced that the power of God was
theirs, such that by stretching forth their hand in faith it
became the hand of the Almighty (see Acts 4:30). Likewise, in a revelation to Edward Partridge "the Lord God,
the Mighty One of Israel," said: *"I will lay my hand upon
you by the hand of my servant Sidney Rigdon,* and you
shall receive my Spirit, the Holy Ghost, even the Comforter, which shall teach you the peaceable things of the
kingdom" (D&C 36:1-2, italics added).

The promise of the Lord that the gospel was restored
"that every man might speak in the name of God the
Lord" (D&C 1:20) finds partial fulfillment in the privilege
granted even the youthful priest, who, in the ordinance of
baptism, acts in the first person for all three members of
the Godhead. Calling the candidate for baptism by name,
he utters these words: "Having been commissioned of
Jesus Christ, I [note that the officiator speaks in the first
person, dramatizing that the power is independent within
himself, even as Peter said, "Such as I have, give I thee"]
baptize you *in the name of the Father, and of the Son, and
of the Holy Ghost. Amen."* (D&C 20:73, italics added.)
And as it is with baptism, so in principle it is with all the
ordinances of the gospel—the bearer of the priesthood,
having an investiture of authority, acts on behalf of his
divine principal.

As it is with the performance of ordinances, so also in
regard to the working of miracles. The Lord Jehovah, the
Eternal God, was born of Mary and lived as the mortal
Jesus. He came in his Father's name and in his own right,
and when he performed miracles he acted in all the majesty of his own divine calling. When Jesus was in Peter's
home in Capernaum, preaching to a crowd of people, four
men removed the tile from the roof and lowered a paralytic
on his couch of pain to the ground before the Master.
Christ then said: "Son, thy sins be forgiven thee." Know-

ing that none but God can forgive sins, the attendant scribes raised the awful spectre of blasphemy. Jesus responded by asking whether it was easier to tell someone his sins were forgiven or to heal the sick. Then he said: "That ye [scribes] may know that the Son of Man hath power on earth to forgive sins"—and he turned to the one whose limbs had no strength—"Arise, and take up thy bed, and go thy way into thine house." (Mark 2:5-11.) And it was done even as he spoke. That this same right, this same spiritual authority, is enjoyed by those who hold his priesthood, is evidenced in the words of James: "Is any sick among you? let him call for the elders of the church; and let them pray over him, anointing him with oil in the name of the Lord; and the prayer of faith shall save the sick, and the Lord shall raise him up: and if he have committed sins, they shall be forgiven him" (James 5:14-15).

Jesus is Jehovah, and Jehovah is God, and God works miracles in his own right and needs neither the name nor the power of another. In contrast, Peter—as with all those who are agents of the Lord Jesus—acted and operated and was authorized by the name above all other names, the name of Jesus Christ. And as it is with speaking, so it is in regard to acting—the agent must be fit, must be worthy, must be in the condition to serve and represent his eternal principal. Mormon wrote: "We know our record to be true, for behold, it was a just man who did keep the record —for he truly did many miracles in the name of Jesus; and *there was not any man who could do a miracle in the name of Jesus save he were cleansed every whit from his iniquity*" (3 Nephi 8:1, italics added; compare D&C 50:26-30). Indeed, those who qualify for the spirit of prophecy and revelation gain that hope and unshaken faith which distills upon the individual as power from on high, a supernal power described by Jacob: "We truly can command in the name of Jesus and the very trees obey us, or the mountains, or the waves of the sea" (Jacob 4:6).

Witnesses of the Name of Christ

To stand as a witness of Christ is to bear testimony of his divine sonship—that he is literally the Son of the Everlasting Father, the offspring of an almighty being; that he inherited from that eternal sire the powers of immortality, the powers to live forever, to defy death; and that by inheritance he received the powers to work out the infinite and eternal atoning sacrifice. To stand as a witness of Christ is to believe and affirm that "salvation was, and is, and is to come, in and through the atoning blood of Christ, the Lord Omnipotent" (Mosiah 3:18). It is to teach and testify that Christ "hath abolished death, and hath brought life and immortality to light through the gospel" (2 Timothy 1:10).

It is one thing to stand as a witness of Christ in the sense that we attest to all men that he is the Son of God and that he was crucified for the sins of the world. But it adds a new dimension to this testimony to say we stand as *witnesses of the name of Christ*. Our witness becomes one of proclaiming his divine sonship and of preaching that salvation comes only to those who believe his gospel, join his Church, live his law, and take his name upon them. Thus it is that the Twelve Apostles are called to be "special witnesses of the name of Christ in all the world" (D&C 107:23; see also 27:12). That is to say, the Twelve are not simply to proclaim that Jesus is the Christ—as critically needed as that witness is today—but also to declare that the path to salvation is through The Church of Jesus Christ of Latter-day Saints, declared by God himself as "the only true and living church upon the face of the whole earth" (D&C 1:30).

This is the pattern for all the Saints—each one in his sphere and place, standing as a witness of the name of Jesus Christ. To stand as a witness of Jesus is to preach that he is Lord and Savior and that salvation is in him and in none other. To stand, further, as a witness of the name of Christ in our day is to complement that messianic witness with a testimony of the Restoration—to preach and proclaim that Christ the Lord has called Joseph Smith, Jr., as the prophet of the Restoration; that priesthoods and keys and powers have been delivered to earth through him by angelic ministrants; that the ordinances of salvation are available once again after a long night of apostasy; that salvation is to be had through The Church of Jesus Christ of Latter-day Saints, a divine organization upon which the Savior has placed his name and authority; and that men and women may come unto Christ through his gospel, ministered through his Church, by his chosen servants.

Conclusion

To act in the name of the Lord is a sacred trust. It is deserving of solemn and ponderous thought. One wonders if we would not preach more gospel doctrines and bear more fervent testimonies if we had fixed in our minds the weighty fact that the words spoken are not ours alone, but they are the words of him whom we represent, him from whom we have received a heavenly authorization. And one wonders if we speak or pray without inspiration, if we teach for doctrine the views and vagaries of men, if we act or perform anything flippantly or lightly—and do it all in the sacred name of our Lord and Savior—one wonders whether we are not taking the name of the Lord in vain.

Jesus, as the agent of Elohim, was engaged in his Father's business. We have a like appointment, and our divine commission includes this provision: ''Wherefore, as ye are agents, ye are on the Lord's errand; and whatsoever ye do according to the will of the Lord is the Lord's business'' (D&C 64:29).

Chapter 6

Worship in His Name

True worshippers shall worship
the Father in spirit and in truth;
for the Father seeketh such to
worship him. For unto such hath
God promised his Spirit. And they
who worship him, must worship in
spirit and in truth.
—JST, John 4:25-26

The most important duty of man is to worship his God in a spirit which befits His majesty and omnipotence. True and saving worship is accomplished only by those who know their God—know his character, attributes, and perfections—and seek to harmonize their wills and their lives with that of the heavens. Only those whose eyes are single to the divine glory, who have chosen to yield their hearts to God and acknowledge and submit to his grander purposes, enjoy the sweet fruits of worship—those transforming and regenerating powers of the Spirit which eventually make mankind like him who gave them life and extends to them the hope of life everlasting.

The Nature of Worship

All of us are the spirit children of the Father. We lived with him in a premortal existence. We have gazed upon his face and heard his voice. Now we live in another time and in another sphere—known to us as the second estate—with the scriptures and the prophets and the Spirit to whisper understanding concerning our life before. The veil of forgetfulness, however, is not completely impermeable. Many of those born into mortal circumstances which do not allow a knowledge of the saving gospel or the receipt of essential ordinances feel after that which is righteous and seek to harmonize their lives with that which is infinite. "Without teaching or training," President Spencer W. Kimball has observed, "man inclines toward the infinite. It seems to be as integral a part of his nature as breathing or eating."

> If the instinctively religious man is in darkness and cannot perceive and know the True and Living God, he will then select and elevate to godship such things as he considers supernatural and super powerful. The river overflows its banks causing loss of life and property and the savage will name it a god and worship and propitiate it with sacrifices. The mountain belches forth smoke, gases and rivers of molten lava and the native calls it god and throws into the seething, boiling volcano a beautiful maiden or an innocent child to appease the wrath of this god. Or he may fashion of wood or stone or marble or of precious metals a god before whom he will kneel and worship.
>
> And so it is fundamental in the life of man to worship and to have a god on whom he may bestow adoration and to whom sacrifices may be offered. (*Teachings of Spencer W. Kimball,* p. 2.)

True worship involves, among other things, fear or reverence toward the Transcendent One; submission and resignation to the will of the Omniscient One; acknowledgment of the hand of the Almighty One; deference to the ways and means of the Infinite One; adoration of the Exalted One; and praise and exultation to the Gracious One.

"Deity is worshiped in prayer, song, sermon, and testimony," wrote Elder Bruce R. McConkie; "by the making of covenants, offering of sacrifices, performance of ordinances, and the participation of religious rituals and ceremonies; he is worshiped by man's act of believing divine truths, by his being converted to them in their fulness; he may be worshiped in thought, word, and deed. But the most perfect of all worship comes from those who first believe the gospel, who then participate in its outward forms, and who finally keep the standards of personal righteousness that appertain to it." (*Mormon Doctrine,* p. 849.)

Worship of the Father

God the Eternal Father is the ultimate object of our worship. In a revelation given at the time of the organization of the restored Church, the Lord explained that "by these things"—by virtue of that which is found in the Book of Mormon and in modern revelation—"we know that there is a God in heaven, who is infinite and eternal, from everlasting to everlasting the same unchangeable God, the framer of heaven and earth, and all things which are in them; and that he created man, male and female, after his own image and in his own likeness, created he them; and gave unto them commandments that they should love and serve him, the only living and true God, and that *he should be the only being whom they should worship*" (D&C 20:17-19, italics added; compare Matthew 4:10).

Indeed, from the beginning men have been commanded to call upon the Father in the name of the Son (see Moses 5:8). Moses, having discerned the craftiness of the father of lies, declared: "Get thee hence, Satan; deceive me not; for God said unto me: Thou art after the similitude of mine Only Begotten. And he also gave me commandments when he called unto me out of the burning bush, saying: Call upon God in the name of mine Only Begotten, and worship me." (Moses 1:16-17.) The great Book of Mormon prophet-theologian Jacob taught:

> We labor diligently to engraven these words upon plates, hoping that our beloved brethren and our children will

receive them with thankful hearts, and look upon them that they may learn with joy and not with sorrow, neither with contempt, concerning their first parents.

For, for this intent have we written these things, that they may know that we knew of Christ, and we had a hope of his glory many hundred years before his coming; and not only we ourselves had a hope of his glory, but also all the holy prophets which were before us.

Behold, *they believed in Christ and worshiped the Father in his name, and also we worship the Father in his name.* (Jacob 4:3-5, italics added; compare 2 Nephi 25:16; D&C 18:40.)

God the Eternal Father is our God and he is Christ's God. The plan of salvation is the plan of the Father, the "gospel of God" (Romans 1:1-3). He is the author and finisher of our faith in the ultimate sense. Christ's ministry is a ministry of reconciliation—he seeks to reconcile fallen men and women to the Father (see 2 Corinthians 5:18-20). Christ glorified the Father (see John 17:1, 4), and so must we. The Lord Jesus worshiped the Father and gained salvation, and so must we. He kept the commandments of the Father, prayed to the Father, and sought the guidance of the Father's Spirit in all he did; so must we.

Our blessed Lord came into the world to work out the infinite and eternal atonement whereby immortality and eternal life are brought to pass. But, as a spirit son of the Father, he also came to work out his own salvation. It was necessary that his worship be centered in a being greater than he. Jesus declared to the Samaritan woman at the well that "the hour cometh, and now is, when the true worshippers shall"—note that it is mandatory—"worship the Father in spirit and in truth; for the Father seeketh such to worship him. For unto such hath God promised his Spirit. And they who worship him, must worship in spirit and in truth." (JST, John 4:25-26.) True Saints worship the Father in the name of the Son by the power of the Holy Ghost.

Worship of the Son

The scriptures attest that "in addition to worshiping the Father, our great and eternal Head, by whose word men are, there is a sense in which we worship the Son. We pay divine honor, reverence, and homage to him because of his atoning sacrifice, because immortality and eternal life come through him. He does not replace the Father in receiving reverence, honor, and respect, but he is worthy to receive all the praise and glory that our whole souls have power to possess." (Bruce R. McConkie, *The Promised Messiah*, p. 566.) Nephi thus wrote that the scriptures, the words of the prophets, teach us "the right way." "For the right way," he continued, "is to believe in Christ and deny him not; for by denying him ye also deny the prophets and the law. And now behold, I say unto you that the right way is to believe in Christ, and deny him not; and Christ is the Holy One of Israel; wherefore ye must bow down before him, and *worship him with all your might, mind, and strength, and your whole soul;* and if ye do this ye shall in no wise be cast out." (2 Nephi 25:28-29, italics added.)

One of the greatest revelations ever given to man was received on 6 May 1833, a portion of which contained valuable truths found in a record of John the Baptist. Quoting from that revelation the words of John, we read as follows:

> And I, John, saw that he [Jesus] received not of the fulness at the first, but received grace for grace;
> And he received not of the fulness at first, but continued from grace to grace, until he received a fulness;
> And thus he was called the Son of God, because he received not of the fulness at the first.
> And I, John, bear record, and lo, the heavens were opened, and the Holy Ghost descended upon him in the form of a dove, and sat upon him, and there came a voice out of heaven saying: This is my beloved Son.
> And I, John, bear record that he received a fulness of the glory of the Father;

And he received all power, both in heaven and on earth, and the glory of the Father was with him, for he dwelt in him.

And it shall come to pass, that if you are faithful you shall receive the fulness of the record of John.

I give unto you these sayings that you may understand and know how to worship, and know what you worship, that you may come unto the Father in my name, and in due time receive of his fulness.

For if you keep my commandments you shall receive of his fulness, and be glorified in me as I am in the Father; therefore, I say unto you, you shall receive grace for grace. (D&C 93:12-20, italics added.)

Certain doctrinal considerations relating to the above passage are vital to our understanding of how we worship. First, true and proper worship of the Father and the Son is associated with service to our fellowmen. John observed that Jesus did not possess the fulness of the glory of the Father from the beginning of his mortal life, but rather that he developed, as do we all, in line-upon-line fashion. Our Lord received "grace for grace"—he was endowed and blessed freely of the Father as he gave himself selflessly to the service of and sacrifice for his brothers and sisters. Second, Christ advanced and progressed, as we all may, "from grace to grace," or, as the Prophet Joseph Smith stated, "from one small degree to another, and from a small capacity to a great one; from grace to grace, from exaltation to exaltation." (*Teachings of the Prophet Joseph Smith,* pp. 346-47.) Thus we can—like our Exemplar—come "in due time" to receive the fulness of the Father.

Christ's pathway to godhood, as described in D&C 93, is also man's pathway to godhood: Jesus the Christ literally "marked the path and led the way, and every point defines" (*Hymns,* 1985, no. 195). The Lord gave this portion of the revelation to us that we might "understand and know how to worship" and that we might know what (or whom) we worship. True worship of the Son consists of emulation of the Son. True and saving worship of the Lord

Jesus consists of imitation of the deeds and acts of the Lord Jesus. We honor those we imitate, those we emulate, those whom we designate as our exemplars.

To worship Christ is to seek to be guileless as Christ is guileless; to be tender and gracious as he is; to be holy as he is. "Ye shall be holy," Jehovah commanded ancient Israel, "for I the Lord your God am holy" (Leviticus 19:2). To worship Christ is to keep the commandments as Christ kept them. It is to make Christ our standard and our model. "How do we worship the Lord? We do it by going from grace to grace, until we receive the fulness of the Father and are glorified in light and truth as is the case with our Pattern and Prototype." (Bruce R. McConkie, *The Promised Messiah,* p. 569.) Christ is worshiped in what we do and how we live. "It is ten thousand times ten thousand things," Elder McConkie testified. "It is keeping the commandments of God. It is living the whole law of the whole gospel. To worship the Lord is to be like him until we receive from him the blessed assurance: 'Ye shall be even as I am.' " (In Conference Report, October 1971, p. 169.)

Prayer in His Name

Even as an exalted, resurrected, and glorified being, Jesus Christ continued to pray to his Father, doing so in words of such grandeur that they could not be uttered or written. Of one such occasion among the Nephites, Mormon wrote:

> And it came to pass that when they [the little children] had all been brought, and Jesus stood in the midst, he commanded the multitude that they should kneel down upon the ground.
>
> And it came to pass that when they had knelt upon the ground, Jesus groaned within himself, and said: Father, I am troubled because of the wickedness of the people of the house of Israel.

And when he had said these words, he himself also knelt upon the earth; and behold he prayed unto the Father, and the things which he prayed cannot be written, and the multitude did bear record who heard him.

And after this manner do they bear record: The eye hath never seen, neither hath the ear heard, before, so great and marvelous things as we saw and heard Jesus speak unto the Father;

And no tongue can speak, neither can there be written by any man, neither can the hearts of men conceive so great and marvelous things as we both saw and heard Jesus speak; and no one can conceive of the joy which filled our souls at the time we heard him pray for us unto the Father. (3 Nephi 17:13-17.)

We are commanded to pattern our prayers after his. Further, we are commanded to pray to the Father in his name. "And whatsoever ye shall ask the Father in my name," he said, "which is right, believing that ye shall receive, behold it shall be given unto you" (3 Nephi 18:20). In fact, if there had been no atonement; if Christ had not given himself as a ransom for sin; if the sinless Son of Man had not chosen to serve as Mediator between an infinite Father and his finite children—if these things were not, prayer unto the Father would be of no avail. Prayer is efficacious because of the intercession of the Son.

The prophet Zenos prayed: "Yea, thou art merciful unto thy children when they cry unto thee, to be heard of thee and not of men, and thou wilt hear them. Yea, O God, thou hast been merciful unto me, and heard my cries in the midst of thy congregations. . . . And thou didst hear me because of mine afflictions and my sincerity; and *it is because of thy Son that thou hast been thus merciful unto me,* therefore I will cry unto thee in all mine afflictions, for in thee is my joy; for *thou hast turned thy judgments away from me, because of thy Son.*" (Alma 33:8-9, 11, italics added.) Likewise the prophet Zenock prayed: "Thou art angry, O Lord, with this people, because they will not understand thy mercies which thou hast bestowed upon them because of thy Son'' (Alma 33:16). And thus it was that Amulek, drawing upon the witness of these prophetic predecessors from the brass plates, taught the faithless Zoramites: ''Therefore may God grant unto you, my brethren, that ye may begin to exercise your faith unto repentance, that ye begin to call upon his holy name, that he would have mercy upon you; yea, cry unto him for mercy; for he is mighty to save'' (Alma 34:17-18).

Let us stop and ponder. We are to pray in the name of Jesus Christ. What does it mean? Is it not the same as with miracles and ordinances and prophesying and preaching? All are done in his name. When we pray in Christ's name, among other things, we put ourselves in his place and stead. We say the words he would say, because our prayers, when they meet the divine standard, are spoken by the power of the Holy Ghost. And because they are spoken in the name of the Blessed Jesus, our words become his words; they are what he would say in the same situation. Hence the revelations instruct: ''And if ye are purified and cleansed from all sin, *ye shall ask whatsoever you will in the name of Jesus and it shall be done.* But know this, *it shall be given you what you shall ask.''* (D&C 50:29-30, italics added; compare 3 Nephi 19:24.)

Those Saints who pray in his holy name, by the power of the Spirit, often find their words reaching beyond their thoughts. They speak words that are not their own. As President Marion G. Romney observed, they know they have spoken under divine direction because they learn things from what they have said. They receive answers to their prayers because they pray for that which they ought, that which God would have them receive. ''I will bless thee forever,'' the Lord said to Nephi, son of Helaman, ''and I will make thee mighty in word and in deed, in faith and in works; yea, even that *all things shall be done unto thee according to thy word, for thou shalt not ask that which is contrary to my will''* (Helaman 10:5, italics added). Truly, "he that asketh in the Spirit asketh according to the will of God; wherefore it is done even as he asketh" (D&C 46:30).

Conclusion

We worship the Father in all we do, in ten thousand times ten thousand ways—through song and service and sacrifice, through prayers and petitions and praise. We worship the Son through expressions of gratitude and acts of acceptance of his infinite atonement; further, we seek to pattern our lives after his perfect and flawless life. Christ the Lord worshiped the Father and so must we; we worship in the name of the Son in the sense that we worship as he would worship. There can be no doubt that if all the Lord's people—bowing in prayer, seeking the Spirit— realized that in closing their petitions in the name of Jesus Christ they were speaking in behalf of their principal, were standing in the place and stead of the Holy One of Israel, their prayers would come nearer to the intended divine standard. And surely edification and enlightenment and communion with the infinite would be more the order of the day among the Latter-day Saints.

Chapter 7

The Dwelling Place of His Name

> The seed also of his servants
> shall inherit it; and they that
> love his name shall dwell therein.
> —Psalm 69:36

On the Sabbath following the dedication of the Kirtland Temple the Lord Jehovah, the Great I AM, appeared to Joseph Smith and Oliver Cowdery saying, "I have accepted this house, and *my name shall be here*, and I will manifest myself to my people in mercy in this house. Yea, I will appear unto my servants, and speak unto them with mine own voice, if my people will keep my commandments, and do not pollute this holy house. Yea the hearts of thousands and tens of thousands shall greatly rejoice in consequence of the blessings which shall be poured out, and the endowment with which my servants have been endowed in this house." (D&C 110:7-9; italics added.)

The Lord's people have always been a temple-building people. Directing the construction of a temple in Nauvoo, the Lord said: "Let this house be built *unto my name*, that I may reveal mine ordinances therein unto my people; for I deign to reveal unto my church things which have been kept hid from before the foundation of the world, things that pertain to the dispensation of the fulness of times" (D&C 124:40-41, italics added). Let us now consider the temple and its function as the dwelling place of the holy name.

The Place of the Divine Presence

The promise of God to ancient Israel was that "in all places where I record my name I will come unto thee, and I will bless thee" (Exodus 20:24). The literal sense of the verse is: "Where I cause my name to be remembered" — that is, "Where my people gather to worship in my name" — "there my Spirit, presence, and power will be." In the instance of this text the place of worship is not of moment, be it temple or open altar, be it chapel or mountainside. Surely the power and influence of God is boundless. There is no place in which we cannot invoke his name and receive his blessings.

Yet there are also sacral places, sacred space, permanent locations where the name of the Lord dwells and his presence and power reside. The residence of the Lord is the temple. Anciently the temple, or place of God's presence, was designated as the site where Israel was to seek his blessings and protection (see 2 Chronicles 20:7-9). In our day the Lord has said: "Inasmuch as my people build a house unto me in the name of the Lord, and do not suffer any unclean thing to come into it, that it be not defiled, my glory shall rest upon it; yea, and my presence shall be there, for I will come into it, and all the pure in heart that shall come unto it shall see God. But if it be defiled I will not come into it, and my glory shall not be there; for I will not come into unholy temples." (D&C 97:15-17.)

Among the Lord's people in all ages the purpose of temples has ever been the same. Thus the Kirtland Temple was built in order "that the Son of Man might have a place to manifest himself to his people" (D&C 109:5). In the dedicatory prayer, Joseph Smith implored our Eternal Father, asking that "thy glory may rest down upon thy people, and upon this thy house, which we now dedicate to thee, that it may be sanctified and consecrated to be holy, and that thy holy presence may be continually in this house; and that all people who shall enter upon the threshold of the Lord's house may feel thy power, and feel constrained to acknowledge that thou hast sanctified it, and that it is thy house, a place of thy holiness" (D&C 109:12-13).

The Place Where the Mysteries of Godliness Are Manifest

"Build a house to my name," came the command of the Lord to Joseph Smith at Nauvoo, "for the Most High to dwell therein. For there is not a place found on earth that he may come to and restore again that which was lost unto you, or which he hath taken away, even the fulness of the [blessings of the] priesthood" (D&C 124:27). Indeed, the higher priesthood, Joseph Smith taught us, "is the channel through which all knowledge, doctrine, the plan of salvation and every important matter is revealed from heaven" (*Teachings of the Prophet Joseph Smith,* pp. 166-67). The Melchizedek Priesthood, or the holy order of God, holds "the key of the mysteries of the kingdom, even the key of the knowledge of God." Such knowledge is obtained through priesthood ordinances. Indeed, we are told that it is in the ordinances that "the power of godliness is manifest." (D&C 84:19-20.)

Expanding this thought, another great revelation on the priesthood states: "The power and authority of the higher, or Melchizedek Priesthood, is to hold the keys of all the spiritual blessings of the church—to have the privilege of receiving the mysteries of the kingdom of heaven, to have the heavens opened unto them, to commune with the general assembly and church of the Firstborn, and to enjoy the communion and presence of God the Father, and Jesus the mediator of the new covenant" (D&C 107:18-19).

Such knowledge and power have been enjoyed by the servants of God in all ages (see D&C 124:39). Prior to the completion of the Kirtland Temple the Lord said: "I gave unto you a commandment that you should build a house, in the which house I design to endow those whom I have chosen with power from on high; for this is the promise of the Father unto you; therefore I command you to tarry, even as mine apostles at Jerusalem" (D&C 95:8-9). It is in the ordinances of the temple that a man and his wife may receive the promise that "Ye shall come forth in the first resurrection . . . and shall inherit thrones, kingdoms, principalities, and powers, dominions, all heights and depths." Indeed, those faithful couples sealed by the Holy Spirit of Promise are assured that "they shall pass by the angels, and the gods," set to guard the way and assure that no unclean thing attempts to enter the presence of the Lord. Theirs is the promise of "exaltation and glory in all things, as hath been sealed upon their heads, which glory shall be a fulness and a continuation of the seeds forever and ever. Then shall they be gods, because they have no end; therefore shall they be above all, because all things are subject unto them. Then shall they be gods, because they have all power, and the angels are subject unto them." (D&C 132:19-20.)

Such was the doctrine that elicited this promise from the resurrected Lord to those of the meridian day: "And to him who overcometh, and keepeth my commandments unto the end, will I give power over many kingdoms; and he shall rule them with the word of God; and they shall be in his hands as the vessels of clay in the hands of a potter; and he shall govern them by faith, with equity and justice, even as I received of my Father" (JST, Revelation 2:26-27). The Revelator called those receiving this promise kings and priests and prophesied that those having so obtained would come from every kindred, tongue, people, and nation (see Revelation 1:5-6; 5:9-10). These servants of God, he said, would be sealed in their foreheads, that is they would have the Father's name written on their foreheads, meaning that they had received the fulness of the priesthood and the assurance of all powers and dominions in the world to come (see Revelation 7:3; D&C 133:18).

The Place of His Authority

For the Lord to place his name upon someone is for him to grant authority or power to them. Of the angel sent to guide the children of Israel in their wilderness wanderings the Lord said: "My name is in him" (Exodus 23:21), meaning "My power and my authority are his." A messenger who comes in the stead of the Lord is deserving of the same reverence and respect that would be accorded the Lord. It is not suggested that we worship the messenger, but rather that we give full attention to the source of the message. "Whether by mine own voice," the Lord declared, "or by the voice of my servants, it is the same" (D&C 1:38). As the Lord has called and ordained those who are to represent him, so he has designated and consecrated certain places where his authority is to be fully manifest.

Well before the children of Israel entered into the promised land it was revealed that a temple was to be built there in which the Lord could "cause his name to dwell" (Deuteronomy 12:11). Thereafter the temple was referred to as a house for "the name of the Lord" (see 1 Kings 3:2; 5:5; 8:16-20, 29). When the temple was built and dedicated, the Lord appeared to Solomon and told him that He had hallowed the temple "to put [His] name there for ever; and mine eyes and mine hearts shall be there perpetually" (1 Kings 9:3; 2 Chronicles 7:16). We would not understand such a text to mean that the God of Israel was forever confined within the walls of Solomon's temple. Rather, as long as there were those laboring in the temple upon whom the Lord had placed his name—priesthood holders empowered to officiate in the ordinances of the house of the Lord and perform its sacred rites—for all intents and purposes God was present, for as his voice becomes one with his servants so do his eyes and his heart.

With the restoration of the gospel in this dispensation came again the command to build a temple "unto my holy name" (D&C 124:39; 105:33; 109:2-5). And again came the promise that in this house of holiness the Lord would place his name upon those who covenanted to be his people (D&C 109:26). Of this principle Elder Dallin H. Oaks observed:

> All of these references to ancient and modern temples as houses for 'the name' of the Lord obviously involve something far more significant than a mere inscription of his sacred name on the structure. The scriptures speak of the Lord's putting his name in a temple because he gives authority for his name to be used in the sacred ordinances of that house. That is the meaning of the Prophet's reference to the Lord's putting his name upon his people in that holy house. (See D&C 109:26.)
>
> Willingness to take upon us the name of Jesus Christ can therefore be understood as willingness to take upon us the authority of Jesus Christ. According to this meaning, by partaking of the sacrament we witness our willingness to participate in the sacred ordinances of the temple and to receive the highest blessings available through the name and by the authority of the Savior when he chooses to confer them upon us. (In Conference Report, April 1985, p. 103.)

The Place Where We Take His Name Upon Us

"I bow my knees," wrote the Apostle Paul, "unto the Father of our Lord Jesus Christ, of whom the whole family in heaven and earth is named" (Ephesians 3:14-15). The familial bonds known to us on earth are but an extension of the heavenly order of things. All that takes place on earth that is right—that is good and proper—is patterned after the order of heaven and will be known to and enjoyed by all who obtain an eternal inheritance there. Describing that future day a revelation declares: "That same sociality which exists among us here will exist among us there, only it will be coupled with eternal glory, which glory we do not now enjoy" (D&C 130:2). It is in the temple that sealing power is exercised to bind husband and wife together for eternity and to tie them to their righteous kindred of generations past and to their children and their children's children to all generations of time. In the temple we "bind together the living and the dead," declared President John Taylor, "in fraternal and patriarchal relations, according to the holy order which exists with the Gods" (from the dedicatory prayer of the Logan Temple; cited in Lundwall's *Temples of the Most High,* p. 91).

This holy and eternal order can be entered into only by those who have through obedience merited adoption into the family of our Father. Such become heirs of God, joint-heirs with Christ, of all the powers and glories of heaven. Heirship "does not come from church membership alone, but admission into the church opens the door to such high status, if it is followed by continued faith and devotion" (McConkie, *Mormon Doctrine,* p. 745). Those to whom such promises are made are known to us as the church of the Firstborn. "Those who become the sons of God in this life are the ones who by enduring in continued righteousness will be gods in eternity" (see *Mormon Doctrine,* pp. 139, 745).

This promise of heirship granted to faithful couples is the crowning ordinance of the temple. These are they who have "overcome by faith, and are sealed by the Holy Spirit of promise, which the Father sheds forth upon all those who are just and true. They are they who are the church of the Firstborn. They are they into whose hands the Father has given all things—they are they who are priests and kings, who have received of his fulness, and of his glory; and are priests of the Most High . . . wherefore, as it is written, they are gods, even the sons of God—wherefore, all things are theirs, whether life or death, or things present, or things to come, all are theirs and they are Christ's, and Christ is God's." (D&C 76:53-59.) These are they who will be called by his name in the last day.

When we partake of the sacrament we renew the covenant made in the waters of baptism. We "witness" that we are willing to take his name upon us (see D&C 20:77-79). Elder Dallin Oaks has explained that we have not actually taken his name upon us at this point but rather witness our willingness to do so. (In Conference Report, April 1985, p. 105.) That is, we have announced our righteous desires, we have entered into a covenant with God, but we have not yet obtained; ours is but a candidacy for exaltation. When the time comes that we have received the fulness of temple blessings or, even more perfectly, when the time comes that we have actually obtained our exaltation, then in the full and perfect sense we have taken his sacred name upon us.

The Place of Eternal Promises

In ancient thought one's name was inextricably bound up with existence. To be nameless was to be without existence. "Personal existence is regarded as continuing posthumously in the name which is perpetuated by a man's descendants. To cut off a name, therefore, is to end the existence of its bearer" (*Interpreters Dictionary of the Bible*, 3:501). Thus we find Saul entreating David in these words: "Swear now therefore unto me by the Lord, that thou wilt not cut off my seed after me, and that thou wilt not destroy my name out of my father's house" (1 Samuel 24:21). Similarly, Bildad describes the state of the wicked by saying: "His roots shall be dried up beneath, and above shall his branch be cut off. His remembrance shall perish

from the earth, and he shall have no name in the street.''
(Job 18:16-17.) Thus during the great millennial reign the
righteous obtain the promise that their seed and their name
shall remain (see Isaiah 66:22).

The gospel contains no greater promises than the continuation of a man's name, the continuation of the family
unit in the worlds to come and the attendant promise of an
endless seed. A graphic illustration of this power as it was
expressed to the ancients comes from the pen of Isaiah.
"Neither let the eunuch say, Behold, I am a dry tree. For
thus saith the Lord unto the eunuchs that keep my sab-
baths, and choose the things that please me, and take hold
of my covenant; even unto them will I give in mine house
and within my walls a place and a name better than of sons
and of daughters: I will give them an everlasting name,
that shall not be cut off" (Isaiah 56:3-5). Thus we look for
a future day when the limitations of mortality are to be
stripped away and all the powers associated with the name
of our Lord and Master are to be enjoyed by those willing
to accept them.

Conclusion

Of necessity the restoration of the gospel requires the
building of temples, for the Lord's people are not to be
without a place in which God can manifest himself, nor are
they to be without a place where his name can perpetually
dwell. Only within this sacral space do men have the privilege, in the full and complete sense, of taking upon themselves the name of Christ and becoming heirs of God and
joint-heirs with his most loved Son. It is in the temple, the
holy mount, the place where heaven and earth meet, that
we receive the fulness of the priesthood and the promise of
the fulness of all gospel blessings.

Chapter 8

Taking His Name in Vain

> Thou shalt not take the name of
> the Lord thy God in vain; for the
> Lord will not hold him guiltless
> that taketh his name in vain.
> —Exodus 20:7

Of the ten commandments given to Moses on Sinai, none is held in greater disregard in the Christian world than the divine injunction that we not take the name of the Lord our God in vain. Further, none of the great commands that have echoed from Sinai have been or are less understood, even by those professing to give heed to them, than is the simple injunction to avoid profaning the sacred name. All who profess that name are required by that declaration to understand the obligations associated with it. To that end let us first define, from the perspective of scripture, the meaning of *in vain, profane,* and *blaspheme.* Having done so we will be in a position to more clearly identify the responsibility associated with taking upon ourselves the name of Christ.

Vain: Its Roots and Scriptural Meaning

The English word *vain* comes from the Latin word *vanus,* meaning "empty" (Shipley, *Dictionary of Word Origins,* p. 373). Its use in the biblical phrase "in vain" is peculiar and may constitute the only occasion in the English language in which *vain* is used as an adverb. It is an adjective in common usage. Contextually it describes that which is worthless or of no substance, value, or importance. Secondary definitions include: fruitless, unreal, ostentatious, light, false, deceitful, not genuine, and spurious. (*Webster's 1828 Dictionary,* 2:105.) In scripture that which is "vain" is either empty and devoid of meaning, as in the worship of idols, or useless and without purpose, as in repetitive and thoughtless prayers (Richards, *Expository Dictionary of Bible Words,* p. 608).

The Hebrew word translated *vain* in the Decalogue carries the idea of emptiness or falsehood. "The Third Commandment (second for Lutherans and Roman Catholics) deals with the use of Yahweh's name *in vain* for that which lacks reality or truth. The name of God expresses his character and power. To call upon unreality, i.e., that which is not an expression of the divine character, by means of the divine name is to use the name *in vain.* Not only perjury but also the practice of magic, which constitutes the invocation of ultimate powers with whom God stands in conflict, and the invocation of the dead, were in all probability among the specific prohibitions implied by this commandment at its inception." (*Interpreter's Bible,* 5:983.)

To Profane: Its Roots and Scriptural Meaning

The word *profane* means "that which was outside the temple [Latin *pro,* before, outside, + *fanum,* temple]" (Shipley, p. 284). To profane is to defile, pollute, or desecrate that which is holy or worthy of reverence. It is to do that which would be unworthy of heaven's blessing or out of harmony with the divine plan. One authoritative source suggests that "the original use of the word may have been in reference to sexual relations, since it is used of Reuben's defilement of his father's line (Gen. 49:4) or of intercourse within the near kin relations forbidden by law. Such actions were considered fornication and prostitution. The word may therefore be used of any action which controverts God's planned order.'' (Harris, Archer, Waltke, *Theological Wordbook of the Old Testament*, p. 289.)

The metaphor most often used in the Old Testament to depict the covenant which God had made with Israel is that of marriage. Thus when Israel sinned against that covenant, seeking alliance with the gods of their pagan neighbors, their infidelity was called fornication and adultery, for a sacred covenant had been profaned.

The principle is best illustrated with the doctrine of the scattering and gathering of Israel. The Lord explained to Ezekiel, a prophet of captivity, the reason why the nation of Israel was destroyed and its people taken into captivity: ''When the house of Israel dwelt in their own land, they defiled it by their own way and by their doings: their way was before me as the uncleanness of a removed woman. Wherefore I poured my fury upon them for the blood that they had shed upon the land, and for their idols wherewith they had polluted it: and I scattered them among the heathen, and they were dispersed through the countries: according to their way and according to their doings I judged them.''

The Lord then explained that in their dispersion they profaned his holy name, for it was an embarrassment for him to have placed his name upon a people unworthy of his protection, a people in bondage. People would say of them, ''These claim to be the Lord's people and yet they have been dispersed from the land that he is said to have given them.'' Thus the Lord said that out of ''pity'' for his holy name he would preserve and gather them.

Ezekiel was directed:

> Therefore say unto the house of Israel, Thus saith the Lord God; I do not this for your sakes, O house of Israel, but for mine holy name's sake, which ye have profaned among the heathen, whither ye went.

And I will sanctify my great name, which was profaned among the heathen, which ye have profaned in the midst of them; and the heathen shall know that I am the Lord, saith the Lord God, when I shall be sanctified in you before their eyes.

For I will take you from among the heathen, and gather you out of all countries, and will bring you into your own land.

Then will I sprinkle clean water upon you, and ye shall be clean: from all your filthiness, and from all your idols, will I cleanse you.

A new heart also will I give you, and a new spirit will I put within you: and I will take away the stony heart out of your flesh, and I will give you an heart of flesh.

And I will put my spirit within you, and cause you to walk in my statutes, and ye shall keep my judgments, and do them.

And ye shall dwell in the land that I gave to your fathers; and ye shall be my people, and I will be your God. (Ezekiel 36:17-28.)

To Blaspheme: Its Scriptural Meaning

To blaspheme is to speak ill of God, his power, or his agents. Several Hebrew words have been translated "blasphemy": *naqab,* meaning "to utter a curse against" (Leviticus 24:11, 16); *gadap,* meaning "to revile" (2 Kings 19:6, 22; Psalm 44:16); but the word that is closest to the New Testament usage and which captures the fullest meaning of the concept of blasphemy is *na as,* meaning "to spurn or treat with contempt" (Richards, p. 129). Illustrations of blasphemy in the Old Testament include disputing God's power (2 Kings 19:4), desecrating his name (Isaiah 52:5), violating his glory (Ezekiel 35:12), and participating in rituals unworthily (Isaiah 66:3). New Testament examples include evil speaking against the Lord's anointed (Acts 6:11), resisting God's will (1 Timothy 6:1; James 2:5-7), and bringing his church into disrepute (Romans 2:22-24).

Defiling the Sacred Name

Having before us a basic idea of what is meant by taking the name of the Lord in vain, profaning that which comes from him, and the nature of blasphemy, let us, with a perspective that is perhaps broader than that usually employed, consider the most serious ways in which the name of Deity is defiled.

1. *The refusal to bow the knee to God and acknowledge him as our Maker and the source of our salvation.* In a marvelous latter-day revelation on the nature of proper worship we are told that "in nothing doth man offend God, or against none is his wrath kindled, save those who confess not his hand in all things, and obey not his commandments" (D&C 59:21). All who have the law of the gospel revealed to them "must obey the same" if they would obtain the rewards. There is no option here. The blessings of salvation are not open to negotiation. No one can reject the covenant of salvation and enter into the Lord's glory. (See D&C 132:3-4.) "If ye will not abide in my covenant," the Lord said, "ye are not worthy of me" (D&C 98:15). No one has the right to refuse honor and reverence to that God who gave us life. True, it is agency that allows us the opportunity to eschew the sacred, yet such actions cannot and will not go unexcused. God will not be mocked. All men are to be judged by their works.

Stubbornness does not call forth the blessings of heaven. It has been said that we cannot break the commandments of God; we can only break ourselves against them. Eventually all must choose whether they will follow that spirit by which the children of Israel walked through the Red Sea on dry ground or that spirit which baptized the pursuing army of Egypt with the baptism of damnation.

2. *The worship of idols.* As we have seen, the term translated "vain" in the Decalogue ranges in meaning from "empty" to "false." The adverbial expression carries the general meaning, "for an empty or false purpose." The condemnation of idol worship is no less relevant today

than it was when written by the finger of the Lord on Sinai. In his proclamation of the latter-day restoration the Lord described those who had strayed from his ordinances and broken the covenant: "They seek not the Lord to establish his righteousness, but every man walketh in his own way, and after the image of his own god, whose image is in the likeness of the world, and whose substance is that of an idol, which waxeth old and shall perish in Babylon, even Babylon the great, which shall fall" (D&C 1:16).

Paul prophetically described our day as one in which men would be "lovers of their own selves, covetous, boasters, proud, blasphemers, disobedient to parents, unthankful, unholy, without natural affection, trucebreakers, false accusers, incontinent, fierce, despisers of those that are good, traitors, heady, highminded, lovers of pleasures more than lovers of God;" and all this, he said, would be done in a "form of godliness," while "denying the power thereof" (2 Timothy 3:3-5).

3. *The breaking of oaths and covenants.* In the context of the Old Testament there were two broad categories of oaths: promissory and assertory. "In a promissory oath, God may be called upon to be a witness to the promise and to act as a judge of performance. God was expected to enforce the provisions of the oath either through the acts of the injured party or through extraordinary means if the injured party were powerless to act. In an assertory oath, God may be called upon to be a witness to the veracity of a person's testimony and, as the reader of the heart, the punisher of lies. One would be taking the divine name in vain if one swore by God to the veracity of false testimony or to the performance of deeds that one did not intend to or was not able to fulfill." (Patrick, *Old Testament Law,* p. 48.)

All ordinances of salvation, indeed all gospel ordinances, are administered in the name of Christ. Nothing can be done for the salvation of man in any other name or by any other authority. The composite of "all covenants, contracts, bonds, obligations, oaths, vows, performances, connections, associations, or expectations," associated with spiritual things constitutes the "new and everlasting covenant" (D&C 132:6-7). To willingly or ignorantly violate that covenant or any of its component parts is to take the name of the Lord in vain. "Hearken and hear, O ye my people, saith the Lord and your God, ye whom I delight to bless with the greatest of all blessings, ye that hear me; and ye that hear me not will I curse, that have professed my name, with the heaviest of all cursings" (D&C 41:1).

The gravity of sin is in proportion to the understanding of the transgressor. Surely it is a greater sin for one who has been baptized to profane the Sabbath day than for one who has not promised to live by gospel standards. Immorality in any form is offensive to the heavens. When commited by one who has made sacred covenants in the house of the Lord, however, it is appreciably more grievous than the same transgression when committed by those who have made no such covenants. Indeed, it is a double sin for the children of the covenant to walk after the ways of the world, for with their transgressions also comes the responsibility of having profaned that sacred name by which salvation comes, that name which they have promised to honor.

4.*Using the name of the Lord without authority.* "For behold," the Lord declared, "verily I say, that many there be who are under this condemnation, who use the name of the Lord, and use it in vain, having not authority" (D&C 63:62). "Although a man should be baptized an hundred times it availeth him nothing" (D&C 22:2), save it is done by one having authority.

> Will I accept an offering, saith the Lord, that is not made in my name?
>
> Or will I receive at your hands that which I have not appointed?

And will I appoint unto you saith the Lord, except it be by law, even as I and my Father ordained unto you, before the world was?

I am the Lord thy God; and I give unto you this commandment—that no man shall come unto the Father but by me or by my word, which is my law, saith the Lord.

And everything that is in the world, whether it be ordained of men, by thrones, or principalities, or powers, or things of name, whatsoever they may be, that are not by me or by my word, saith the Lord, shall be thrown down, and shall not remain after men are dead, neither in nor after the resurrection, saith the Lord your God. (D&C 132:9-13.)

In all societies and among all peoples, to act falsely in someone else's name is a serious wrongdoing. Be it in the form of plagiarism, counterfeiting, forgery, or even blasphemy, such acts are offensive to the spirit of truth. Many have mistakenly professed the authority to teach the gospel of Christ and administer the ordinances of salvation, but notwithstanding their sincerity, this is a grievous offense against the kingdom of God. Those who would usurp the sacred right to teach the gospel or administer its ordinances; who have not been properly called, ordained, and sent forth by him whose gospel it is and yet profess to act in his holy name, do so without authority—their works are vain. They are administering adulterated truths, doctrinal forgeries, and counterfeited ordinances. However well intended, their works are profane, lacking validity in this life and, as the Lord himself declared, without "efficacy, virtue, or force in and after the resurrection from the dead" (D&C 132:7).

5. *Teaching false doctrine.* Jeremiah described the latter-day gathering of Israel as a time when those who had been spiritually awakened would come unto the Lord from the ends of the earth, saying: "Surely our fathers have inherited lies, vanity, and things wherein there is no profit. Shall a man make gods unto himself, and they are no

gods?'' Because these noble souls are honest truth seekers, the Lord declared: "Therefore, behold, I will this once cause them to know, I will cause them to know mine hand and my might; and they shall know that my name is The Lord." (Jeremiah 16:19-21.) Jeremiah described the corruption of the scriptures taking place in his own day, saying: "How do ye say, We are wise, and the law of the Lord is with us? Lo, certainly in vain made he it; the pen of the scribes is in vain." (Jeremiah 8:8.) *The New English Bible* renders the verse thus: "How can you say, 'We are wise, we have the law of the Lord,' when scribes with their lying pens have falsified it."

In his prophetic description of the churches of the last days, Nephi wrote: "Yea, and there shall be many which shall teach after this manner, false and vain and foolish doctrines, and shall be puffed up in their hearts, and shall seek deep to hide their counsels from the Lord; and their works shall be in the dark" (2 Nephi 28:9). So great would be the influence of "vain and foolish doctrines," Nephi prophesied, that "all" will have gone astray "save it be a few, who are the humble followers of Christ; nevertheless, they [the true believers in Christ] are led, that in many instances they do err because they are taught by the precepts of men" (2 Nephi 28:14).

6. *Religious hypocrisy.* In every form of evil, hypocrisy has played its part. "The seducer must swear false oaths, the deceiver feign friendship, the tyrant profess care for the commonwealth" (Hastings, *Dictionary of Christ and the Gospels,* 1:766). Among the religious the wolf wears sheep's clothing, speaking, as the Psalmist said, vanity with smooth lips and a double heart (Psalm 12:2). Of such were the Pharisees of Jesus' day, of whom he said: "Ye made the commandment of God of none effect by your tradition" (Matthew 15:6). Ritual had supplanted righteousness among these critics of the Savior, whose outward display of devotion was not matched with inward purity. "Ye make clean the outside of the cup and of the platter, but

within they are full of extortion and excess" (Matthew 23:25).

To the Pharisees of all ages the spirit of truth inquires: "To what purpose is the multitude of your sacrifices unto me? saith the Lord: I am full of the burnt offerings of rams, and the fat of fed beasts; and I delight not in the blood of bullocks, or of lambs, or of he goats. When ye come to appear before me, who hath required this at your hand, to tread my courts? Bring no more vain oblations. . . . I am weary to bear them . . . I will hide mine eyes from you: yea, when ye make many prayers, I will not hear: your hands are full of blood." (Isaiah 1:11-15.)

The revelations of the Restoration are no less express in denouncing vain religion. "I, the Lord, have looked upon you," he told the infant church in this dispensation "and have seen abominations in the church that profess my name." (What better way, might we ask, could one find to disguise evil than in the name of the Lord!) This, the Lord said, had "given the adversary power," but he assured us that "such shall be reclaimed; but the hypocrites shall be detected and shall be cut off, either in life or in death, even as I will." Then comes the ever-important warning: "Wherefore, let every man beware lest he do that which is not in truth and righteousness before me." (D&C 50:4-9.)

As to the time of recompense that surely must come, the Lord has promised: "Vengeance cometh speedily upon the inhabitants of the earth, a day of wrath, a day of burning, a day of desolation, of weeping, of mourning, and of lamentation; and as a whirlwind it shall come upon all the face of the earth, saith the Lord. And upon my house shall it begin, and from my house shall it go forth, saith the Lord; first among those among you, saith the Lord, who have professed to know my name and have not known me, and have blasphemed against me in the midst of my house, saith the Lord." (D&C 112:24-26.)

7. *Bringing the Church into disrepute.* We join with James in asking of those who have taken upon themselves

the sacred name of Christ and then not lived worthy of their covenants: "Do not they blaspheme that worthy name by the which [they] are called?" (James 2:7). Latter-day Saints have come to expect that when a member of the Church is involved (or even suspected of having been involved) in some improper activity that is reported by the news media, considerable fuss will invariably be made of the fact that he is a member of the Church. From the days of its organization there have been those who have delighted in bringing to the Church whatever embarrassment is possible. Surely for us to give them license to do so is to profane the sacred and to hinder the work of the Lord.

8. *Perjury.* To ancient Israel the Lord said: "Ye shall not swear by my name falsely, neither shalt thou profane the name of thy God: I am the Lord" (Leviticus 19:12). The concern of the Mosaic law was not to eradicate the custom of taking oaths but rather to impress upon the people the sacred nature of their doing so. Honesty, loyalty to God, and the truths of salvation, were to stand supreme among the Lord's people. They were expressly forbidden to bear false testimony or to swear by false gods.

Without truth there can be no society, no order among men. Anciently an oath was a means of impressing the necessity of truth and integrity upon parties to an agreement or upon witnesses in an investigation. That obligation was fortified by holy words and sacred acts intended to bring a sense of confidence and assurance to those involved. Thus the legal procedure, of which an oath was a part, was closely associated with sacred places, was administered by holy persons, and was sealed by the invocation of the name of Deity. To perjure such an oath was indeed a very serious matter and was not to go unpunished (see Ezekiel 17:13, 16, 18-19).

Christ, in his charge to his newly chosen Apostles, forbade the swearing of oaths. "Swear not at all," he said, "neither by heaven; for it is God's throne: nor by the earth; for it is his footstool: neither by Jerusalem; for it is the city of the great King. Neither shalt thou swear by thy head, because thou canst not make one hair white or black. But let your communication be, Yea, yea; Nay, nay: for whatsoever is more than these cometh of evil." (Matthew 5:34-37.)

This restriction on taking oaths may have been imposed because of some rabbinical interpretations which made the taking of oaths a matter of trickery and deceit. If, for instance, a person had bound himself "by Jerusalem," he was obligated to honor his oath unless he was not actually facing Jerusalem when he took it (see Richards, p. 461). An oath by the temple or the altar might be broken without sin, but not an oath by the gold of the temple, or by the gift on the altar, if they had been dedicated to the service of God (see Matthew 23:16). To eliminate such untruthfulness, the Savior simply advocated that a man's word be his bond. If a man said that something was so, it was so; if he said he would do a thing, it mattered not what direction he was facing, he should do it. For those who have taken upon themselves the name of Christ, to do less than this surely constitutes profanity.

9. *Evil speaking of the Lord's anointed.* "Let no corrupt communication proceed out of your mouth" Paul counseled the Saints of the meridian day, "but that which is good to the use of edifying, that it may minister grace unto the hearers. And grieve not the holy Spirit of God, whereby ye are sealed unto the day of redemption. Let all bitterness, and wrath, and anger, and clamour, and evil speaking, be put away from you, with all malice." (Ephesians 4:29-31.) In a similar vein we have been admonished to strengthen our fellow Saints in all our conversation, in all our prayers, in all our exhortations, and in all our doings (see D&C 108:7).

Satan, the shameful name borne by the prince of darkness, means "adversary," or "accuser." He is described in the book of Revelation as "the accuser of our brethren" who was "cast down" (see Revelation 12:10), thus describing the role he played in the preearth councils as one who spoke evil of those whom the Father of our spirits had chosen to bear his name and be his spokesmen. As is to be expected, those who have chosen the adversary as their father in this estate identify themselves as the accusers of the Lord's anointed. To those who partake of that spirit, the word of the Lord declares:

> Cursed are all those that shall lift up the heel against mine anointed, saith the Lord, and cry they have sinned when they have not sinned before me, saith the Lord, but have done that which was meet in mine eyes, and which I commanded them.
>
> But those who cry transgression do it because they are the servants of sin, and are the children of disobedience themselves.
>
> And those who swear falsely against my servants, that they might bring them into bondage and death—
>
> Wo unto them; because they have offended my little ones they shall be severed from the ordinances of mine house.
>
> Their basket shall not be full, their houses and their barns shall perish, and they themselves shall be despised by those that flattered them.
>
> They shall not have right to the priesthood, nor their posterity after them from generation to generation.
>
> It had been better for them that a millstone had been hanged about their necks, and they drowned in the depth of the sea.
>
> Wo unto all those that discomfort my people, and drive, and murder, and testify against them, saith the Lord of Hosts; a generation of vipers shall not escape the damnation of hell. (D&C 121:16-23.)

10. *Becoming sacrilegious and irreverent.* Literally "a *sacrilegious* person is one that steals *sacred* things" (Shipley, p. 308). It is the "filching or the befouling of the sacred" (*Interpreters Dictionary of the Bible,* 4:159). It also embraces "the unworthy or irreverent use of sacred persons, places, or things" (*Webster's 1828 Dictionary,* p.

1996). In Old Testament times the classic illustration of sacrilege was that of the Seleucid tyrant Antiochus IV who, having stolen the sacred utensils of the temple, ordered the sacrifice of swine and other unclean animals upon its altar (1 Macabees 1:21-53). Yet, no sacrilege exceeds that of the Jewish rejection and vile mistreatment of their Messiah. Christ was ridiculed, scorned, mocked, spat upon, and scourged before being offered up in an ignominious death upon the cross. Indeed, the "trial of cruel mockings and scourgings, . . . bonds and imprisonment" (Hebrews 11:36) has been the common lot of prophets in all ages and among all peoples.

"Fools mock," the scripture declares, "but they shall mourn" (Ether 12:26). As to those within the faith, the Lord has warned that they shall "trifle not with sacred things" (D&C 6:12), and always "remember that that which cometh from above is sacred, and must be spoken with care, and by constraint of the Spirit" (D&C 63:64). Thus there is to be no light-mindedness when we meet together in the Savior's name. Those of spiritual refinement cannot help but be offended when that which is sacred is treated frivolously or flippantly. It would be difficult to imagine the Spirit of the Lord being enticed to attend such a meeting or remaining had that Spirit already been present. Jokes or clever stories are a poor substitute for the teaching of the gospel or the testimony of Christ.

The commandment given those who attended the school of the prophets was to "cease from all your light speeches, from all laughter, from all your lustful desires, from all your pride and light-mindedness, and from all your wicked doings" (D&C 88:121); no other spiritual attitude could be expected to open the heavens and bring the desired outpouring of the Spirit. Surely this is the spirit that reigns whenever those we sustain as prophets, seers, and revelators meet, and this constitutes the example of the spirit that ought to prevail whenever we meet in the sacred name of Christ. Indeed, the command to the Saints of the last days is to leave Babylon, cleanse themselves from sin, and then gather in "solemn" assemblies, that every man might "call upon the name of the Lord" (D&C 133:5-6).

It need not be supposed that the spirit that ought to prevail when we meet in the name of Christ is antithetical to that of a cheerful heart and a glad countenance. The spirit of the gospel is inseparable from the spirit of rejoicing. Yet our worship services are not the place for "much laughter," for the Lord said, "this is sin" (D&C 59:15). Surely humor, smiles, and laughter are all to be found in heaven and are equally welcome in our meetings. It is the calculated, the exaggerated, the irreverent, however, that is offensive to the Spirit. For instance, it is unfortunate that the idea should exist that testimony or gospel teaching need be prefaced with a joke among the Saints. Can we imagine the Sermon on the Mount beginning with a joke, or how trivialized the revelations in the Doctrine and Covenants would be if each was prefaced with an attempt at humor? Likewise the ever-present stories of "St. Peter and the pearly gates," wherever these are told, are not only irreverent but also bad doctrine, for "the keeper of the gate is the Holy One of Israel; and he employeth no servant there" (2 Nephi 9:41).

None had a more intimate relationship with Deity than did the Son of God, yet all his references to the Father evidence a profound and reverential sense of deference. He was equally respectful of the prophets who had preceded him and whom he frequently quoted. In the same vein, given that the revelations declare that the likes of Abraham, Isaac, and Jacob have gone on to that ennobled status above and beyond man, have entered into their exaltation, "and sit upon thrones, and are not angels but are gods" (D&C 132:37), we ought to speak of them and their names with the highest of dignity and respect, and thus not trivialize their labors or ministries with shallow and uninspiring stories.

Gospel covenants and gospel truths are to be treated with the utmost reverence. "The mysteries of the kingdom ye shall keep within yourselves," Jesus instructed the meridian Twelve, "for it is not meet to give that which is holy unto the dogs; neither cast ye your pearls unto swine, lest they trample them under their feet. For the world cannot receive that which ye, yourselves, are not able to bear; wherefore ye shall not give your pearls unto them, lest they turn again and rend you." (JST, Matthew 7:10-11.)

In all our worship we are to "serve God acceptably with reverence and godly fear" (Hebrews 12:28). Before his throne "all things bow in humble reverence, and give him glory forever and ever" (D&C 76:93). "Holy and reverend is his name" (Psalm 111:9). "Reverence is due not only to God and his holy name," wrote Elder Bruce R. McConkie, "but to his laws, his gospel, his covenants, his prophets, his ordinances, his temples, his priesthood, and all the things he has revealed and given for the salvation and blessing of his children" (*Mormon Doctrine*, p. 651).

11. *Using profane speech.* The revelation of Sinai declared profaning the name of Deity a capital offense. In the book of Leviticus we read that the son of an Israelitish woman "blasphemed the name of the Lord, and cursed. And they brought him unto Moses. . . . And the Lord spake unto Moses, saying, Bring forth him that hath cursed . . . and let all that heard him lay their hands upon his head, and let all the congregation stone him. And thou shalt speak unto the children of Israel, saying, Whosoever curseth his God shall bear his sin. And he that blasphemeth the name of the Lord, he shall surely be put to death, and all the congregation shall certainly stone him." (Leviticus 24:11, 13-16.)

Commenting on this story, President Gordon B. Hinckley observed:

> While that most serious of penalties has long since ceased to be inflicted, the gravity of the sin has not changed.

The Lord has spoken again in our time concerning this serious matter. In the revelation given to President Brigham Young on January 14, 1847, while the Saints were preparing to leave Winter Quarters for these valleys in the West, the Lord said to them, Keep yourselves from evil to take the name of the Lord in vain, for I am the Lord your God, even the God of your fathers, the God of Abraham and of Isaac and of Jacob (D&C 136:21).

In a general epistle to the entire Church issued by the First Presidency on April 8, 1887, a hundred years ago, they said concerning this problem, which evidently was serious then as it is now, "The habit . . . which some young people fall into, of using vulgarity and profanity . . . is not only offensive to well-bred persons, but it is a gross sin in the sight of God, and should not exist among the children of the Latter-day Saints." (Conference Report, October 1987, pp. 56-57.)

"Do angels take the Lord's name in vain?" asked Elder George Q. Cannon.

The idea is so ridiculous that we scarcely like to ask the question. . . . How dare we do that which angels dare not do? Is it possible for us to argue that that which is forbidden in heaven is praiseworthy on earth?

Though we are sure no boy can tell us any advantage that can arise from the abuse of God's holy name, yet we can tell him many evils that arise therefrom. To begin, it is unnecessary and consequently foolish; it lessens our respect for holy things and leads us into the society of the wicked; it brings upon us the disrespect of the good who avoid us; it leads us to other sins, for he who is willing to abuse his Creator is not ashamed to defraud his fellow creature; and also by so doing we directly and knowingly break one of the most direct of God's commandments. (*Juvenile Instructor*, 27 September 1883, p. 156.)

It is strange indeed that many people choose their clothes with the greatest of care that they might represent themselves well, and then they undress their minds and souls with grubby speech. Though we seek not to make a man an offender for a word, it ought to be observed that even the best of thoughts inappropriately expressed seem very much out of place. Though few realize what they are saying, grubby words include the likes of "gad," "Egad," "gosh," "golly," and "gee," each of which is a euphemism for the name of Deity and fails to show the dignity and respect due the Supreme Being. We could hardly imagine such language being used to implore the blessings of heaven or to teach saving truths. Like see-through cloth, too, they fail to give the wearer appropriate modesty of expression. Similarly "darn it," and "dang" (euphemisms for "damn"), though not entirely crude and offensive, are never wholly acceptable among people of spiritual refinement.

12. *Blaspheming against the Holy Ghost.* Of all sins of which man is capable, none is greater than that of blasphemy against the Holy Ghost. So grevious is this sin that it is without forgiveness in this world or the world to come (see Matthew 12:31–32). To blaspheme against the Holy Ghost is to have a perfect knowledge—a knowledge obtained by the opening of the heavens, a knowledge of the verity of the gospel and the reality of God and his Only Begotten Son—and then to deny that knowledge with full accountability and to come out in open warfare against the Lord and his anointed servants. "You cannot save such persons," the Prophet Joseph Smith declared (*Teachings of the Prophet Joseph Smith,* p. 358).

Conclusion

To treat God, or that which properly bears his name, with disdain or contempt cannot be less than a serious sin. That which profanes the sacred may be born of ignorance, disbelief, or hypocrisy. In any case it is offensive to the spirit of light and truth; conversely, it is attractive to the spirit of darkness and error. Each spirit brings with it its own train of attendants. "That which is of God is light; and he that receiveth light, and continueth in God, receiveth more light; and that light groweth brighter and brighter until the perfect day" (D&C 50:24). Those whose "minds have been darkened by unbelief" because they have "treated lightly" the manifestations of heaven are "under condemnation"; theirs is the promise of a scourge and judgment, for they have polluted that which is holy (see D&C 84:54-59).

Of those who rejected his claim to messiahship in the meridian day, the Savior said: "This people draw nigh unto me with their mouth and honoureth me with their lips; but their heart is far from me. But in vain they do worship me, teaching for doctrine the commandments of men." (Matthew 15:8-9.) In so saying the Lord authenticates and carries forward the words of Isaiah in which the ancient prophet spoke of vain worship born of the traditions of men by which it was thought possible to gain the favor of God without moral obedience (see Isaiah 29:13).

These same words were spoken again by the Lord in response to the question of the youthful Joseph Smith when he asked which of the religious sects of this day he should join. Of the religions of our modern day the Lord said they have a "form of godliness, but they deny the power thereof," (Joseph Smith-History 1:19). As in the meridian day, this emphasis of form without substance will not satisfy either salvational requirements or the God who established them. Now as then, it partakes of the sin of taking the Lord's name in vain.

In His Name and in None Other

There is none other way nor name
given under heaven whereby man
can be saved in the kingdom of God.
—2 Nephi 31:21

The week before Easter, Christians celebrate what has come to be known as Palm Sunday, commemorating the triumphal entry of Jesus the Christ into Jerusalem before his crucifixion and death. Matthew records that "a very great multitude spread their garments in the way; others cut down branches from the trees, and strawed them in the way. And the multitudes that went before, and that followed, cried, saying, Hosanna to the Son of David: Blessed is he that cometh in the name of the Lord; Hosanna in the highest." (Matthew 21:8-9.) But this Spirit-inspired refrain was more than a shout of praise to the King Emmanuel, more than a nation's testimony that Jesus of Nazareth was their Messiah; it was a plea for deliverance to the Lord of Hosts. *Hosanna* means literally, "save O Lord; save we pray" (compare Psalm 118:25-26). Indeed, he that came in the name of the Lord—in the name of his Father, the Almighty Elohim—brought power to deliver, power to redeem, power to save. Christ is the way to salvation, the way to the Father, and thus eternal life was and is and is to come in and through his holy name and in no other way.

The Gospel of God the Father

The plan of salvation is that system, ordained by God himself, whereby his children may advance through the different stages of their existence to the point where they become even as he. This "great plan of happiness," called also the "plan of redemption," is the "gospel of God" (Romans 1:1-3) and was taught by God the Father and introduced to his children ages before the second estate began. Joseph the Prophet explained that "God himself, finding he was in the midst of spirits and glory, because he was more intelligent, saw proper to institute laws whereby the rest could have a privilege to advance like himself. . . . He has power to institute laws to instruct the weaker intelligences, that they may be exalted with himself so that they might have one glory upon another." (*Teachings of the Prophet Joseph Smith,* p. 354.)

In the grand council of heaven Elohim put forth the question: "Whom shall I send?" (Abraham 3:27.) We should be quick to observe that the question was not "What shall I do?" or "Does anyone have any suggestions?" or "How shall we get things rolling?" The very question implies a plan or program clearly understood by all in attendance—by all the hosts of heaven, all the sons and daughters of the Eternal Father. The real issue was the person to serve as the chief advocate of the plan. By extension the Father's question would thus be: "Whom shall I send to be my Son? Who will go down and work out the infinite and eternal atoning sacrifice? Who will be mine Only Begotten in the flesh?" It was on that pristine occasion that Jehovah, the firstborn spirit child of Elohim, responded: "Here am I, send me" (Abraham 3:27). Also: "Father, thy will be done, and the glory be thine forever" (Moses 4:2).

In discussing the Savior's simple but poignant words, President John Taylor wrote: "From these remarks made by the well beloved Son, we should naturally infer that in the discussion of this subject the Father had made known His will and developed His plan and design pertaining to these matters, and all that His well beloved Son wanted to do was to carry out the will of His Father, as it would appear had been before expressed. He also wished the glory to be given to His Father, who, as God the Father, and the originator and designer of the plan, had a right to all the honor and glory." (*The Mediation and Atonement,* p. 94.) In reality there was only one plan from the beginning—the plan of the Father. Jehovah became its chief proponent and Lucifer its arch antagonist.

Because Jehovah, who became Jesus Christ, was the one selected to have the Father's name placed upon him; because Christ was appointed to become the "lamb slain from the foundation of the world"; because Jesus would come to earth, take a mortal body through a mortal woman, but also receive the powers of immortality from his exalted Father; and because Christ would be the one chosen to work out the awful atonement and thereby ransom fallen men from the grasp of Satan and from the effects of temporal and spiritual death—because of all these things, the plan of the Father, the gospel of God, came to be known as the gospel of Jesus Christ. The Father's name became his name, and the Father's gospel became his gospel.

Faith in the Name of Christ

To have faith in the name of Christ is to have faith in his plan, which is the plan of the Father. It is to accept Jesus as Lord and acknowledge his ability, and his alone, to draw all men unto him, to forgive their sins and cleanse their souls, as well as to raise their rotting corpses from the graves in glorious immortality. To have faith in the name of Christ is to learn of him, to listen to his words, to study his life and seek to emulate the only perfect being ever to walk the earth. Joseph Smith taught that the plan of salvation is indeed a "system of faith" which equips men and women to gain that saved nature that is so perfectly characterized

in the sinless one. He declared that "Christ . . . is the prototype or standard of salvation; or, in other words, . . . he
is a saved being, . . . because he is a just and holy being;
and . . . his salvation depends upon his being precisely
what he is and nothing else; . . . for salvation consists in
the glory, authority, majesty, power and dominion which
Jehovah possesses and in nothing else; and no being can
possess it but himself or one like him." (*Lectures on Faith,*
7:9, 17.)

To have faith in the name of Christ is to have an assurance, born of the Spirit, of our Lord's divine sonship, to
know by revelation that no earthly man or woman — no
matter how gifted and no matter how noble — could have
done what He did. His work was and is the work of a god,
and the product of his labors — salvation itself — is available
only because of the merciful intercession of one with power
over life and death.

Salvation by the Grace of Christ

To have faith in the name of Christ is to acknowledge
his hand in all things, to confess that there are labors
beyond the power of man to perform. Man cannot forgive
his own sins any more than he can create himself. Man
cannot cleanse and renew and regenerate the human soul
any more than he can resurrect himself. These are the infinite actions of a god, and they require the intervention of
godly powers in man's behalf. To have faith in the name of
Christ is to recognize and receive the saving grace of
Christ.

The power unto life and salvation is in Jesus Christ, the
person. The power is not in programs, even inspired programs. Programs cannot save. They have not the power to
forgive sins or sanctify or soothe troubled souls. It is the
gospel of Jesus Christ which is "the power of God unto
salvation" (Romans 1:16), a power which derives from
him who is omnipotent. The saints of all ages come to

know by revelation the source of their salvation. They talk of Christ, rejoice in Christ, preach of Christ, prophesy of Christ, and write according to their prophecies, that those of their generation, especially their children, may know to what source they may look for a remission of their sins (see 2 Nephi 25:26; Enos 1:1-8; Mosiah 4:1-3; Alma 36:17-21).

Christianity without the living Christ is at best deficient. Righteousness without the Righteous One cannot redeem. Theology without the gospel lacks the power of salvation. In speaking of the limitations of the Law of Moses—the inability of the type (the Law) to have saving power without the antitype (the Lawgiver)—Abinadi preached with great authority to the priests of King Noah: "And now ye have said that salvation cometh by the law of Moses. I say unto you that it is expedient that ye should keep the law of Moses as yet; but I say unto you, that the time shall come when it shall no more be expedient to keep the law of Moses. And moreover, I say unto you, that salvation doth not come by the law alone; and were it not for the atonement, which God himself shall make for the sins and iniquities of his people, that they must unavoidably perish, notwithstanding the law of Moses." (Mosiah 13:27-28.) In offering a modern prophetic commentary upon this passage, Elder Bruce R. McConkie taught:

> Now let us suppose a modern-day case. Suppose we have the scriptures, the gospel, the priesthood, the Church, the ordinances, the organization, even the keys of the kingdom—everything that now is down to the last jot and tittle—and yet there is no atonement of Christ. What then? Can we be saved? Will all our good works save us? Will we be rewarded for all our righteousness?
>
> Most assuredly we will not. *We are not saved by works alone, no matter how good; we are saved because God sent his Son to shed his blood in Gethsemane and on Calvary that all through him might ransomed be. We are saved by the blood of Christ.*

To paraphrase Abinadi: "*Salvation doth not come by the Church alone:* and were it not for the atonement, given by the grace of God as a free gift, all men must unavoidably perish, and this notwithstanding the Church and all that appertains to it." ("What Think Ye of Salvation by Grace?", p. 48, italics added.)

Modern revelation, especially the Book of Mormon, reconciles the age-old theological issue of grace vs. works. In the language of Nephi, we are saved by the grace of God, *after all we can do* (2 Nephi 25:23). Jacob thus counseled his people to "reconcile yourselves to the will of God, and not to the will of the devil and the flesh; and remember, after ye are reconciled unto God, that it is only in and through the grace of God that ye are saved" (2 Nephi 10:24). President Joseph Fielding Smith explained that "it is a doctrine of the Church that is fully upheld and sustained by the scriptures, and by the handdealings of God with the children of men from the beginning, that he does not do for us one thing that we can do for ourselves, but requires of us that we do *everything* for ourselves that is within our power for our salvation. I think that is logical and reasonable. On the other hand, the Lord has done everything for us, for our salvation, that we could not do for ourselves, and there were some things that we could not do for ourselves, and we had to have help from an infinite source." (*Doctrines of Salvation* 2:308-9.)

The works of man are necessary for salvation, but they are insufficient of themselves. Moroni pleaded with his readers to "come unto Christ, and be perfected in him, and deny yourselves of all ungodliness; and *if ye shall deny yourselves of all ungodliness, and love God with all your might, mind, and strength, then is his grace sufficient for you,* that by his grace ye may be perfect in Christ; and if by the grace of God ye are perfect in Christ, ye can in nowise deny the power of God" (Moroni 10:32, italics added). Mortal life is a gift of loving parents, a gift which embraces a family name to be honored by living in harmony with the standards of the family. Eternal life, in like manner, is a divine gift, a gift which could never be earned, but rather is *inherited*. It is the greatest of all the gifts of God (see D&C 6:13; 14:7), granted to those who receive and hold in sacred remembrance the family name which they are called upon to honor.

The Name of God in Our Foreheads

As previously discussed, those who qualify to go where gods and angels are, who inherit the highest of eternal possibilities, receive the "seal of God upon their foreheads" —the indelible mark whereby they are everlastingly known and identified as God's own. These "shall see his face; and his name shall be in their foreheads" (Revelation 22:4). After John the Revelator had opened the sixth seal of his panoramic vision—after he had begun to view the doings of man and God during the sixth thousand years of the earth's temporal continuance (see D&C 77:6-7)—he "saw four angels standing on the four corners of the earth, holding the four winds of the earth, that the wind should not blow on the earth, nor on the sea, nor on any tree. And I saw another angel," John wrote, "ascending from the east, having the seal of the living God: and he cried with a loud voice to the four angels, to whom it was given to hurt the earth and the sea, saying, Hurt not the earth, neither the sea, nor the trees, *till we have sealed the servants of our God in their foreheads.* And I heard the number of them which were sealed: and there were sealed an hundred and forty and four thousand of all the tribes of the children of Israel." (Revelation 7:1-4, italics added.)

In interpreting these apocalyptic verses, Elder Bruce R. McConkie wrote that "the everlasting gospel, as restored through Joseph Smith and his associates, is to be preached 'to every nation, kindred, tongue, and people,' during the sixth seal."

But the preaching of the restored gospel in all the world is not by any means the whole story. Converts are to be made everywhere. The same things here shown to John had been revealed more than six centuries before to Nephi. That Hebrew prophet beheld that in the last days the church of the devil would have "dominion over all the earth, among all nations, kindreds, tongues, and people," and that "the church of the Lamb, who were the saints of God, were also upon all the face of the earth." (1 Ne. 14:9-27.)

And now we learn that after the converts are made, . . . there will be those among them who advance and progress until they become kings and priests. See Rev. 1:1-6; 5:1-14; 20:4-6. John here sees 144,000 of these kings and priests, 12,000 from each tribe, converted, baptized, endowed, married for eternity, and finally sealed up unto eternal life, having their calling and election made sure. (*Doctrinal New Testament Commentary*, 3:490-91.)

The Prophet Joseph Smith thus spoke of "four destroying angels holding power over the four quarters of the earth *until the servants of God are sealed in their foreheads, which signifies sealing the blessings upon their heads, meaning the everlasting covenant, thereby making their calling and election sure*." (*Teachings*, p. 321, italics added.) Orson Pratt similarly discoursed upon the meaning and importance of the seal of God in the forehead.

On that occasion he [John] saw one hundred and forty-four thousand standing upon Mount Zion, singing a new and glorious song; the singers seemed to be among the most happy and glorious of those who were shown to John. They, the one hundred and forty-four thousand, had *a peculiar inscription in their foreheads. What was it? It was the Father's name. What is the Father's name? It is God*—the being we worship. If, then, the one hundred and forty-four thousand are to have the name of God inscribed on their foreheads, will it be simply a plaything, a something that has no meaning? Or *will it mean that which the inscriptions specify?—that they are indeed Gods—one with the Father and one with the Son;* as the Father and Son are one, and both of them called Gods, so will all His children be one with the Father and the Son, and they will be one so far as carrying out the great purposes of Jehovah is concerned. (*Journal of Discourses,* 14:242-43, italics added.)

Conclusion

After King Benjamin had given to his people the name of Christ—after the people had agreed by covenant to take upon them the holy name of their Redeemer and vowed thereafter to keep his commandments—the righteous Benjamin concluded with this plea and invitation: "Therefore, I would that ye should be steadfast and immovable, always abounding in good works, *that Christ, the Lord God Omnipotent, may seal you his, that you may be brought to heaven, that ye may have everlasting salvation and eternal life,* through the wisdom, and power, and justice, and mercy of him who created all things, in heaven and in earth, who is God above all" (Mosiah 5:15, italics added). Thus salvation—which is eternal life or exaltation—consists of being sealed to him whose hallowed name we covenant to receive through the new birth and which is granted us with the fulness of the priesthood in holy places.

"Praise Ye His Name"

O Lord our Lord, how excellent is
thy name in all the earth!
—Psalm 8:1

The Lord's people should rejoice in him and sing praises unto his holy name continually. Cries of hosannah and shouts of hallelujah have ever been a part of the lives of the faithful. When we think of what has been revealed in this day in regard to the Holy One of Israel; when we ponder upon the light and truth and power that have been delivered in this the final dispensation of grace—the opening of the heavens in the spring of 1820 and the manifestation of the Father and Son to the youthful Joseph Smith; the coming of a book designed and prepared to bear witness to Jew and Gentile that Jesus is the Christ, affirming anew that his is the only name whereby salvation comes; the appearance of a host of angelic ministrants declaring and restoring their rights, keys, priesthoods, and majesties, all that the knowledge and power of God might be available again on earth—when we consider all these things, our souls should well up with eternal gratitude.

When we reflect upon the fact that living oracles—Apostles and prophets—special witnesses of the name of Christ, walk the earth today; that holy temples, houses upon which he has placed his name, have been erected; and, further, that every man may speak in the name of God the Lord, having that holy name sealed upon him and his posterity through endless generations—when we reflect on these wondrous things we cannot but raise our voices in anthems of praise to the King Emmanuel. Truly our cup is full. Our desires to acknowledge and recognize and praise him who is eternal knows no bounds. As the ancients heralded the triumphal entry of the mortal Messiah to the Jerusalem of old, so the Saints of the latter days herald the millennial Messiah, who shall yet descend with his righteous hosts to the New Jerusalem. We raise our voices in union with the Zion of old in refrains of "Hallelujah, for the Lord God omnipotent reigneth" (Revelation 19:6).

Paul, writing of that transcendently holy name, testified of the "mighty power" which has been wrought through the atoning mission of Jesus Christ, when God "raised him from the dead, and set him at his own right hand in the heavenly places, far above all principality, and power, and might, and dominion, *and every name that is named,* not only in this world, but also in that which is to come" (Ephesians 1:19-21, italics added). He also explained that Christ was made "so much better than the angels, as *he hath by inheritance obtained a more excellent name*" than the angels. "For unto which of the angels said he [God] at any time, thou art my Son, this day have I begotten thee? And again, I will be to him a Father, and he shall be to me a Son?" (Hebrews 1:4-5, italics added.)

He who bore that name which is above all other names, who freely gives that name to his covenant children, also

> thought it not robbery to be equal with God:
> But made himself of no reputation, and took upon him the form of a servant, and was made in the likeness of men:
> And being found in fashion like a man, he humbled himself, and became obedient unto death, even the death of the cross.

Wherefore, *God also hath highly exalted him, and given him a name which is above every name:*

That at the name of Jesus every knee should bow, of things in heaven, and things in earth, and things under the earth;

And that every tongue should confess that Jesus Christ is the Lord, to the glory of God the Father. (Philippians 2:6-11, italics added.)

In like spirit and with a fervor and enthusiasm born of the Spirit, the Psalmist proclaimed: "O Lord our Lord, how excellent is thy name in all the earth! who hast set thy glory above the heavens." (Psalm 8:1.)

In the same spirit enjoyed by the ancients, a modern apostolic witness of the name of Christ is rendered in these poetic words:

The name of Jesus—wondrous name—the name in which the truths of salvation are taught; the name in which the ordinances of salvation are performed; the name in which miracles are wrought, in which the dead are raised and mountains moved;

The name of Jesus—wondrous name—the name by which worlds come rolling into existence; the name by which redemption comes; the name which brings victory over the grave and raises the faithful to eternal life;

The name of Jesus—wondrous name—the name by which revelation comes and angels minister; the name of him by whom all things are and into whose hands the Father hath committed all things; the name of him to whom every knee shall bow and every tongue confess in that great day when the God of Heaven makes this planet his celestial home. (Bruce R. McConkie, *The Promised Messiah*, p. 300.)

John the Revelator beheld "ten thousand times ten thousand, and thousands of thousands" declaring: "Worthy is the Lamb that was slain to receive power, and riches, and wisdom, and strength, and honour, and glory" (Revelation 5:11-12). From one end of heaven to the other the echoing strains acclaim:

Glory to God on high!
Let heaven and earth reply.
Praise ye his name.
His love and grace adore,
Who all our sorrows bore.
Sing aloud evermore:
Worthy the Lamb.
(*Hymns,* 1985, no. 67.)

Thus—in the words of one of our outstanding Latter-day Saint hymns—we sing and we shout with the armies of heaven: "Hosanna, hosanna to God and the Lamb! Let glory to them in the highest be given, henceforth and forever, Amen and amen!"

Bibliography

Bromiley, Geoffrey W. *Theological Dictionary of the New Testament*. Grand Rapids, Michigan: William B. Eerdmans Publishing Co. The Paternoster Press, 1985.

Clark, James R., comp. *Messages of the First Presidency*. 6 vols. Salt Lake City: Bookcraft, 1965-75.

Conference Reports of The Church of Jesus Christ of Latter-day Saints. Salt Lake City: The Church of Jesus Christ of Latter-day Saints, October 1971; October 1973; April 1985; October 1987.

Harris, R. Laird, Gleason L. Archer, and Bruce K. Waltke. *Theological Wordbook of the Old Testament*. Vol. 1. Chicago: Moody Press, 1980.

Hastings, James D., ed. *Dictionary of Christ and the Gospels*. Vol. 1. New York: Charles Scribner's Sons, 1908.

Hymns of The Church of Jesus Christ of Latter-day Saints. Salt Lake City: The Church of Jesus Christ of Latter-day Saints, 1985.

Interpreter's Bible. 12 vols. New York: Abingdon Press, 1952.

Interpreter's Dictionary of the Bible. 5 vols. Nashville: Abingdon Press, 1962.

Journal of Discourses. 26 vols. Liverpool: F. D. Richards & Sons, 1855-86.

The Juvenile Instructor, 27 September 1883.

Kimball, Edward L., comp. *The Teachings of Spencer W. Kimball.* Salt Lake City: Bookcraft, 1982.

Lundwall, N. B., comp. *Temples of the Most High.* Salt Lake City: Bookcraft, 1965.

McConkie, Bruce R. *Doctrinal New Testament Commentary.* 3 vols. Salt Lake City: Bookcraft, 1965-73.

_____. *Mormon Doctrine,* 2nd ed. Salt Lake City: Bookcraft, 1966.

_____. "The Foolishness of Teaching." Address to Church Educational System, August 1981.

_____. *The Promised Messiah.* Salt Lake City: Deseret Book Co., 1978.

_____. "What Think Ye of Salvation by Grace?" *Brigham Young University 1983-84 Fireside and Devotional Speeches.* Provo, Utah: Brigham Young University Publications, 1984.

McConkie, Joseph Fielding. *Gospel Symbolism.* Salt Lake City: Bookcraft, 1985.

The New English Bible, 2nd ed. New York: Oxford University Press, 1971.

Nyman, Monte S. and Robert L. Millet, eds. *The Joseph Smith Translation: The Restoration of Plain and Precious Things.* Provo, Utah: Religious Studies Center, Brigham Young University, 1985.

Patrick, Dale. *Old Testament Law.* Atlanta: John Knox Press, 1985.

Pratt, Orson. *Orson Pratt's Works.* Salt Lake City: Parker Pratt Robison, 1965.

Richards, Lawrence O. *Expository Dictionary of Bible Words.* Grand Rapids, Michigan: Zondervan Publishing House, 1985.

Shipley, Joseph T. *Dictionary of Word Origins.* New York: Philosophical Library, 1945.

Smith. George Albert. *Sharing the Gospel With Others.* Salt Lake City: Deseret Book Co., 1948.

Smith, Joseph. *History of the Church of Jesus Christ of Latter-day Saints,* ed. B. H. Roberts. 7 vols. Salt Lake City: Deseret Book Co., 1957.

_____. *Lectures on Faith.* Salt Lake City: Deseret Book Co., 1985.

Smith, Joseph Fielding. *Doctrines of Salvation,* comp. Bruce R. McConkie. 3 vols. Salt Lake City: Bookcraft, 1954-56.

Smith, Joseph Fielding, comp. *Teachings of the Prophet Joseph Smith.* Salt Lake City: Deseret Book Co., 1976.

Taylor, John. *The Mediation and Atonement of Our Lord and Savior Jesus Christ.* Salt Lake City: Deseret News Co., 1882.

Webster, Noah. *An American Dictionary of the English Language,* reprint, 4th ed. San Francisco: Foundation for American Christian Education, 1985.

Subject Index

performed by servants of God, 43–44
performed in Solomon's temple, 62–63
power of godliness manifest in, 60

– P –

Palm Sunday, significance of, 86
Parents, honoring of, 14
Partridge, Edward, gift of Holy Ghost
given to, 44
Paul, doctrine of adoption taught by, 25
on becoming sons of God, 9
on holy name of Christ, 96
possesser of power through Christ's
name, 12
prophecy on last days, 72
Perdition, 10–11
Perjury, probably prohibited by third
commandment, 68
profanity a form of, 77–78
Peter, authorized by name of Jesus
Christ, 45
healing of lame beggar by, 11–12,
42–43
Pharisees, hypocrisy of, 75–76
Philo, on significance of names, 11
Physical death, introduced by Adam's
fall, 16–17
Plan of salvation, Adam's fall necessary
to, 16–17
taught by God the Father, 51, 87
Power, to act in Christ's name, 42–45
through taking on Christ's name, 12
Power of godliness, manifested through
priesthood ordinances, 60
Pratt, Orson, on importance of God's
seal in foreheads of the righteous,
93–94
on rules and blessings of adoption into
kingdom of God, 18
Prayer, communion with the infinite, 57
efficacious because of Atonement, 55
in name of Jesus Christ, 56–57
of Christ among Nephites, 54–55
Premortal life, plan of salvation taught
to spirits in, 87
Satan's role as accuser in, 78–79
understanding of, 48–49
Priesthood, blessings of, 66
denied to those who accuse the Lord's
anointed, 79
essential to exaltation, 43
spiritual authority of, 45
See also Blessings of priesthood;
Aaronic Priesthood; Melchizedek
Priesthood
Priesthood callings, mantle of authority,
13

Priesthood ordinances, 60
Priests and kings, to receive fulness of
the Father, 64–65
Profane, definition of, 68–69
Profanity, 68–70
punishable by death in time of Moses,
82
spiritual darkness produced by use of,
84–85
Promissory oath, 72

– R –

Rebellion, against God, 10–11
Re-deem, definition of, 17
Redemption, through faith in Jesus
Christ, 18
Rejoicing, in spirit of gospel, 81
Religions, denial of power of God by, 85
Repentance, blessings of Atonement
received through, 18
of Alma the Younger, 33
rule of adoption into kingdom of God,
18
to give "new heart" to penitent Israel,
70
Repetition, of name of Deity, 28
Respect, for Deity and prophets, 81
Responsibility, to teach doctrines of
Jesus Christ, 36–37
Restoration of gospel, 46–47, 95
included command to build temple, 63
Joseph Smith's role as witness in, 2–4
purpose of, 4
Reverence, essential element in teaching
gospel, 80–81
for sacred things, 82
Rigdon, Sidney, instrument in hand of
the Lord, 44
testimony that Jesus lives, 2
Romney, Marion G., on power of prayer,
56

– S –

Sabbath day, 13
profaning of, 73
Sacrament, significance of partaking of,
65
taking name of Jesus Christ through,
63
Sacrifices, pagan, 49
Sacrilege, biblical examples of, 80
Sacrilegious, definition of, 79
Salvation, attainable only through
emulation of Jesus Christ, 89
by grace of Christ, 89

Scripture Index

NEW TESTAMENT

BOOK OF MORMON